ADVANCE PRAIS

"Full of useful tips, a truly encyclopaedic range of references and exercises that will change how you do things."

Sue Unerman, CTO, MediaCom and author of *Belonging: The key to transforming and maintaining diversity, inclusion and equality at work*

"Another masterclass from Muswell Hill's answer to Mark Twain. Tas unlocks everything you need to know about storytelling from 'Once upon a time' right through to 'The End.'"

Richard Swaab, Deputy Chairman, AMV BBDO agency

"Enlightening and witty, *The Storytelling Workbook* is an outstanding build on the first of its series that introduced us to the art and power of a strong narrative. In an age overloaded with data, information and decisions, Tas teaches us how to cut through the noise using key principles for storytelling designed to hook, surprise and delight our audience. True to his passion for behavioural economics, funny and relatable anecdotes and linguistics, Tas has woven these principles into an enjoyable read that inspires action for its reader. This book gives the reader an opportunity to not only understand the importance of each principle, but 'how' they can be practically applied in both our personal and professional worlds. A valuable guide for all marketing and insights professionals who are seeking to deliver more impactful presentations."

Haley Amodeo, Insights Manager, Maple Leaf Foods, Canada

"The framework for the workbook (what you will learn, what you will do, what that will lead to) is thoughtful and exciting. Tas has broken down complicated topics in a way that feels attainable for anyone. He also sets up the reader to embrace their personality and bring that into their storytelling."

Krista Bradley, Senior Market Research Manager, Research and Insight, Microsoft

"A storytelling primer that is relevant to the SAS (short attention span) crowd in being in tune with current events, as well as packed with pop culture and irreverent humour. It's equally relevant for both professional and personal acuity."

Kat Fay, Consumer and Neuromarketing Research Lead, Cleveland Avenue LLC

"Great applications to storytelling for business, pleasure, speeches, presentations or even crafting your CV. Scholarly, thorough and well-researched. Tasgal draws on fields such as neuroscience, psychology, comedy and great literature to provide us with a simple, yet comprehensive guide. A brilliant resource to help you succeed as a storyteller. A masterclass in storytelling."

Graham Shaw, Speaker, coach and author

"I kept thinking how useful it would have been in countless moments in my life in advertising – writing letters to clients, contact reports, agency briefs, presentations, brand reviews and all that kind of stuff – and how much better if I'd had this brilliant *aide memoire*. It is packed with so many useful thoughts, ideas and insights to make the narrative flow, help the reader digest and remember what one has written – it may even have helped in the dating game."

Patrick Mills, Director of Membership and Professional Development, The Institute of Practitioners in Advertising (IPA)

"Think of this book as the Marie Kondo of storytelling. Tas gives practical guidance on how to clear the clutter, amplify your message and clarify your narrative, giving you the tools to tell a story that's engaging. Anyone who can use Douglas Adams, JJ Abrams and De La Soul to illustrate how to tell a story has my vote. Clear and simple guidance littered with relevant, amusing and unusual references to help you do what we all need to do: tell a story in an engaging manner. If you want to tell a story in a more engaging way, remember the rule of three. *Buy it now. Then read it.* And finally? *Put it into practice.*"

James Max, TalkRADIO presenter

"Writing a book about the art of storytelling could tend to the 'dry and science' end of the spectrum if not handled correctly. Tas has written this book with just the right balance of 'skillful and amusing' that will make you want to keep it close at hand for when stuck in the throes of despair about your next presentation/speech/white paper. The book will make you work over the nine weeks, but the journey is delightful and eye-opening."

Tony Spong, Lead Consultant, the AAR group consultancy

"In the digital age more than ever, we need to appreciate that storytelling is what triggers empathy, interaction and sharing. Tas is an insightful and witty writer and in this sequel to *The Storytelling Book*, this workbook goes further in introducing and helping you to apply the techniques and frameworks of storytelling to everything from a student essay, writing a better CV, to telling your brand story or even finding a life-partner."

Katie Zhou, CEO MetaThink Consultancy,
Shanghai, China

"This book is an essential, practical guide for everyday life, be it in the business space or indeed for students and those just starting out in their careers. It is written in an effortless style that makes you feel like you are in conversation with Tas the author; what is particularly helpful is that his nine-week programme includes what each phase will lead to, as well as what you will learn on your path to becoming a great storyteller. The quotes will stay with you and look out for the elephant at the end – just brilliant!"

Louise Whitcombe, Head of Customer Engagement, Ogilvy UK

"Everybody in business seems to be talking about the importance of storytelling, yet very few organizations are paying it more than lip service. Experts in storytelling seem to be happy to make it a black box that only they can unlock. In *The Storytelling Workbook*, Tas opens this black box for all of us. He tells the story of why we are drawn to stories, how we make them our own and how they affect our identity, our behaviour and our influence on others. He uses examples to show us the 'what' of good stories. Backed by science and human history, this makes a delightful and useful read. But the great achievement of this thought-starting and easy-to-read book is the coaching and exercises he gives us on 'how.' How we can create, shape and sustain better stories. How we can make the stories we develop align with and provoke the behaviours we would like the audience to embrace. And that is how stories can have a real impact, not just on your audience, but on your business as well."

Mathew Wilcox, Behavioural Science expert,
author of *The Business of Choice*

"The profound power of storytelling, of how to engage, enthral and energize others with who you are, and why they need to listen to you, is one of the greatest gifts. Learning the skills of great storytelling is an elephantine task. Yet, like the joke of 'How do you eat an elephant?' with the riposte, 'One bite at a time' provides the pathway for this workbook. It is full of helpful step-by-step support, sagacity and sensible advice and guidance for all areas of social interaction – including dating! A really practical, accessible and inspiring tome."

Andy Green, Founder, Grow Social Capital

Published by
LID Publishing
An imprint of LID Business Media Ltd.
The Record Hall, Studio 304,
16–16a Baldwins Gardens,
London EC1N 7RJ, UK

info@lidpublishing.com
www.lidpublishing.com

A member of:

businesspublishersroundtable.com

© Anthony Tasgal, 2022
© LID Business Media Limited, 2022

Printed by Imak Ofset

ISBN: 978-1-912555-97-0
ISBN: 978-1-911671-47-3 (ebook)

Cover design: Matthew Renaudin
Page design: Caroline Li

THE
STORYTELLING
WORKBOOK

ANTHONY TASGAL

A NINE-WEEK PROGRAMME
TO TELL YOUR STORY

MADRID | MEXICO CITY | LONDON
NEW YORK | BUENOS AIRES
BOGOTA | SHANGHAI | NEW DELHI

To everyone who got us through it.

CONTENTS

HOW TO USE
THIS WORKBOOK

With this workbook, the goal is to encourage you to apply the principles and precepts of storytelling across a variety of domains and aspects of your life, both personal and professional.

Hopefully, you will be able to take on the theory and principles and adopt them in practice.

For the exercises that are dotted throughout, you may wish to consider applying them in any or all of these contexts:

- **Presentations:** These don't have to use our old friend PowerPoint (other systems are available, including not using charts at all). I remain a staunch believer that presentations don't have to be just 'one damn chart after the next' (ODCAN), inflicting a numbing listlessness and existential crisis of hope on your audience.
- **Documents:** As above, in the beginning was Word, but it doesn't have to be that way. While *some* written documents have to be written in a formal, often paralyzing style (I'm looking at you, annual report or student essay), the majority of documents could benefit from being enlivened.
- **Speeches:** As someone who does a bit of what is rather flatly labelled 'public speaking,' I can attest to the fact that a daunting majority of people who make speeches

at conferences, events and even educational meetings (I'm thinking Key Stage 3 introductions) could do with a hefty dose of storytelling to counteract the tendency to anaesthetize an audience into docile capitulation.

- **Telling your 'brand story' and marketing communications:** My background in the marketing and marcomms world means that I am especially keen on recommending storytelling techniques for use in creating your brand story. Too often, brands talk like lumbering robots spewing out factful messages swathed in jargonized nuggets of post-rationalized units of persuasion. The world of marketing comms has become more anodyne, anaesthetized and analytical. The burgeoning of Big Data generally would benefit from some of the emotional overlay that storytelling can give everything from internal comms and newsletters to website copy and external communications.
- **You and your CV:** Anyone in need of sprucing up their CV can benefit from some invigorating storytelling.
- **Dating:** Bear with me. This is not the most obvious context perhaps, but beguiling Cupid is a sphere in which finding and telling one's story might lead to true happiness.

So, over the nine weeks of this programme, you will be guided through a mixture of theory and practice. You will learn new ideas and tips, then implement them yourself though a series of exercises.

This is what the programme looks like from the start.

	What you will learn	What you will do	What that will lead to
Week 1: Get Past Attention Spam	How not to be ignored, and not to rely on facts and information	An exercise to ensure you don't get buried in the weeds	Thinking about the virtues of emotions, attention and simplicity
Week 2: Junk the Jargon	To rid your material of as much stale, formal jargon as possible	An exercise that forces you to replace the meaningless with the meaningful	Getting into the right space to apply the SIMPLE principles
Week 3: Be SIMPLE	The six guiding principles of storytelling	Exercises that show the benefits of structure, meaning and memorability	Avoiding ODCAN (one damn chart after the next) and leading towards the importance of structure
Week 4: Weave a Golden Thread	The power of structure and framework	Exercises where you weave your own thread	Having the essential components of storytelling in place
Week 5: Create Conflict	Why you can't have a real story without conflict	Exercises where you design conflict into your document, CV, profile etc.	Being ready to bring in one key emotion
Week 6: Surprise!	Why surprise will help us evade attention spam	An exercise where you inject surprise and witness the results	Preparing for the last three ingredients
Week 7: Grab Them Early	Why how we start (anything) is crucial to its memorability and impact	Exercises where you craft a killer opening line, and imagine a 'what if'	Linking structure with start to create a 'through-line'
Week 8: The Rule of Three	The power of three across all media	An exercise to enable you to practise with 'threes'	Approaching the finish line and preparing the killer headline
Week 9: Here Are The Headlines	Why headlines are concise, elegant and powerful	An exercise where you create the perfect headline	Creating a knockout story based on all of the ingredients above

PROLOGUE

Before we dive into the programme, let's pause to see why all of these disparate domains have one set of factors in common.

This is that we are all swimming (some may be drowning) in a sea of overpopulation – of competition, of people, of facts – or bombarded by a relentless onslaught of rivals. Brands are searching for ways to stand out, job hunters strive to be the most desirable candidates, and presenters and persuaders aim to affect decision-makers in the most effective ways possible.

In all these varied spheres, what sings out loud and clear are the same essential qualities: we need memorability, saliency and differentiation.

Before we start, here is an epigraph for everything that follows. This is quite possibly my favourite quotation of all time (note: my children will inform you that that is about as reliable a measure as 'my favourite band of all time'):

> I have made this letter longer than usual because
> I have not had time to make it shorter.

Though attributed to everyone from Mark Twain (one of the great quote magnets) to Benjamin Franklin, and even back to the Roman statesman, lawyer and speaker Marcus Tullius Cicero, it seems to have originated with the French philosopher Blaise Pascal, in a letter from a collection called *Lettres Provinciales* in the year 1657.

Its timeless truth: that it is incredibly difficult to write something short, concise and pithy, but virtually effortless to write anything long, sprawling and directionless.

One brief caveat.

As a lapsed classicist (anyone who has negotiated their way through my other books must have suspected this by now), I have always been under the sway of the rhetorical counsel of the ancients, notably the likes of Aristotle, Cicero and Quintilian. So, I have retained the broad rubric of 'storytelling,' but much of the thinking is more akin to certain elements of rhetoric and oratory. I have done so because this would have almost certainly remained an unpublished manuscript if I'd called it *The Rhetoric Workbook* and you wouldn't be here now.

A GRAND TOUR OF STORYTELLING

In which we examine a number of quotes and clips, and a variety of endorsements of the storytelling instinct.

Storytelling Is All-Embracing
Let's start with UK talk show host (and now author) Graham Norton, famous for a segment that ends each episode of

The Graham Norton Show (2007–) called the "Red Chair." Here, audience members are invited to sit on the chair and tell a personal story – the more embarrassing the better. If Norton and his celebrity panel are bored or irritated, they pull a lever and the audience member flips back and is tipped over. In a TV documentary, Norton revealed the secrets of a good lever-proof story:

> To have a good story, you need structure.
> And to have that you need three things.
> Solid middle, a great opening and a brilliant ending
> (cue audience story referring to a microscopic male appendage), though not necessarily in that order.[1]

Think about how many talent show programmes (*Britain's Got Talent* or *The X Factor*, for instance) feature the participants' stories. This is a way of giving us access not only to their skills but also to their journeys and goals.

The Mnemonic Power of Storytelling

The human being is a storytelling machine: our self is a story or series of stories that we tell about *ourselves* to construct *our selves*.

Let's explore for a moment how our self, our memory and our stories all interweave and overlap. In doing so, we'll consider some insights from the most famous living psychologists. And let's acknowledge that our memories are not as perfect as we like to think.

Take US Senator Mitt Romney. In 2012, Romney gave a speech in Michigan that many found rather moving. In it, Romney recalled as a child attending a local Golden Jubilee – an event that celebrated the 50th year of the automobile. Romney's father was the grandmaster of ceremonies at the event.

A bit of journalistic archaeology uncovered a teeny-weeny problem: this didn't happen. The Golden Jubilee took place on June 1, 1946, which was about nine months before Romney was born.

How does this happen and what does it stay about our storytelling urge?

Before this, experimental psychologist Elizabeth Loftus designed a series of fiendishly clever experiments. Loftus is currently a professor at the University of California, Irvine, and was the highest ranked woman in a 2002 list of the top 100 living psychological researchers of the 20th century.[2]

In one famous study, Loftus demonstrated the power of priming and framing. Her team showed subjects a clip of a car crash and then asked them how fast one of the cars was going when it 'hit' (or 'smashed into' or 'collided with') the other car. The study found that estimates varied wildly depending on the verb used, suggesting that leading questions (and language) can distort and contaminate memory. This led Loftus to ponder whether it would be possible to implant entirely false memories.[3]

Loftus did not just uncover that it is possible to implant entirely new memories in the brain. She also found that we naturally embrace and embroider them, unknowingly weaving together threads of fantasy and truth that become impossible to disentangle. (More on weaving in Week 4.)

More specifically (and worryingly for those who like to maintain the purity myth of memory), there is ample evidence that information that is acquired after an event can significantly alter the memory of that event. The processes of retrieval and filling in mean that not every telling of an event will be the same, and our copying fidelity will not be as high as we'd like to think. Loftus constantly reiterates her astonishment at the levels of detail that we confabulate and then believe in – what Lauren Slater calls the "confusion between imagination and memory."[4] Confabulate being the technical term for when our brain spins a story to self-justify.

The science seems clear: it is a hard fact that our senses detect something like 11 million pieces of information per second, but our conscious mind can only process around 40 of these. So, making up stories is what we are universally prone to do in order to make sense of who we are (or might want to be).

As Loftus said about Romney:

> When we remember something, we're taking bits and pieces of experience – sometimes from different times and places – and bringing it all together to construct

what might feel like a recollection but is actually a construction. The process of calling it into conscious awareness can change it, and now you're storing something that's different. We all do this, for example, by inadvertently adopting a story we've heard – like Romney did.[5]

British readers may recall former Prime Minister David Cameron announcing in a speech in 2015 that he supported West Ham United, having frequently claimed to be an Aston Villa fan. At the time he attributed this to a "brain fade."[6]

This brings both good and bad news.

On the positive side, it reinforces the contention here that storytelling comes so naturally to us all that it seems perverse to devise tools and styles of presentation that go so severely against it.

On the other hand, it should also come with a warning: to beware the tendency of our brains to confabulate and conflate (or lie) without our conscious knowledge. It also adds weight to the assertions of those who warn us that we are 'unreliable witnesses.' They caution that we are not merely prone to suggestibility but hungry for it, in order to fill in any gaps or inconsistencies in our 'selves' and in our search for a socially validated narrative of who we are.

The Educational Power of Storytelling

One specific domain that needs a significant infusion of storytelling is that of education. I speak (again) as a parent and lecturer when I say that too often the process of education and instruction has been set adrift on a sea of facts, commandments and antediluvian theories of what the Greeks called pedagogy.

A brief interlude now follows.

My daughter was recently studying psychology at the University of Sussex in the quirky, uber-hip 'unofficial gay capital of the UK' – the Portland of the UK's south coast that is Brighton.

Being aware that I had a more than passing interest in that academic subject (specifically in relation to the domain loosely gathered under the title of 'behavioural economics'), she was keen to demonstrate her enthusiasm at every juncture. She would frequently send me pictures of charts from lectures, references to experiments or scientists she knew I was aware of, and other ways of reaching across the intergenerational chasm.

One day, she sent a series of pictures that she had taken in a lecture on neuroscience and the brain, knowing that some of it would resonate with my interest in the topic.

So, first I received a picture of a cross-section of a brain with an arrow pointing at the prefrontal cortex.

Then, shortly after, a picture of the same section, with an arrow marking the amygdala.

A further 30 seconds later and there was another shot, this time of the same image, but here the arrow indicated the hippocampus.

Within seconds, it was the turn of the thalamus to be similarly featured.

At this point, my daughter, myself and you too, dear reader, have got the point. This is one way of delivering a lecture on the different parts of the brain, their specific functions and their interconnections.

But it is not a good way.

Whatever your degree of fanaticism for staring at brain parts, however much lobe-love you display, no matter how much white matter you feel matters or how fervently you celebrate the cerebral, it's important to stop and think. Relentlessly showing one largely identical slide after another and intoning some facts over it may work for the first two or three occasions, but it will fall off a cliff in terms of attention retention very soon after.

The moral: just because *you* think something is giddily fascinating...

We don't need to get embroiled in the 'has our attention span shortened?' question in the era of hyper-information, or even whether 'younger people' (please don't say 'millennials' in my presence) or students suffer from the shortest attention spans on record. For the record, labelling an entire generation with one catch-all definition is sweeping, lazy and inimical to insight. Similarly, frisky young marketing folk are wont to classify whole swathes of the population as the 'over 50s.' Imagine being one of those 'over 50s' yourself: this is one of the most egregious examples of reductionism in marketing. As Richard Dawkins once said, reductionism is all well and good unless you're the one being reduced.[7]

There shouldn't be a need to so ham-fistedly point out the irony that this was someone discussing how the brain works and communicating in a way that is a flagrant breach of understanding how the brain receives communication. However, it is necessary.

So, what should be done (other than sending the attention police to monitor that lecturer's output)?

We will return to the importance of metaphor and analogy in Week 1, but let us give an example here.

Dean Burnett is unusual in being able to call himself a neuroscientist, lecturer, author, blogger, podcaster, pundit and occasional stand-up comedian. The success of his satirical science column in The *Guardian*, "Brain Flapping," led to the publication of two books: *The Idiot Brain* (2016) and *The Happy Brain* (2018). He knows the importance of information and entertainment.

This is how Burnett explains the thalamus. In describing how our brain regulates our body, he first explains – scientifically – that the thalamus connects to the most advanced parts of our brain but also to the more primitive ('reptile') regions. It therefore receives information that is pertinent to our 'fight or flight' instinct. Fair enough. The dry science bit is done and dusted (but not dusty).

But, as a good communicator, Burnett knows not to leave it there (or even point to the thalamus on a... you get the idea). He says:

> If the brain were a city, the thalamus would be the main station where everything arrives before being sent where it needs to be.[8]

Another analogy that Burnett uses concerns the differences between older, more fundamental systems and processes in the body (such as those that regulate our heart rate) and those that are more modern, sophisticated and temperamental (or vulnerable to alcohol). How does he reinforce this contrast? The first category of systems, he says, is a bit like an old Walkman, which you could happily throw down a flight of stairs and still expect it to have a good chance of working. In contrast, he likens the second category to a smartphone – "tap a smartphone on the side of a table and you end up with a hefty repair bill," he says.[9]

One last instance (that pesky rule of three – see Week 8). In his chapter on how the brain engages in the act of perception (spoiler: biology is not technology – it is imperfect and tends to fill in much more than we'd like to admit), Burnett compares the brain to a police sketch artist. This is a nice metaphor, but it's not quite there yet. No, when exploring how the brain is the only organ not to have pain receptors, he delivers this delicious little vignette:

> The brain feeling pain is like calling your own number from your own phone and expecting someone to pick up.[10]

It's eloquent, amusing, insightful and mercifully free of scientific jargon or numbing unintelligibility. There is huge conceptual overlap between humour and insight. They both deal in the 'aha!' – the sound of the penny dropping, the explanatory satisfaction of a discovery.

Let's sign off this section with some words from William James, the American thinker and educator often deemed the father of psychology:

> If the topic be highly abstract, show its nature
> by concrete examples. If it be unfamiliar, trace some
> point of analogy in it with the known. If it be inhuman,
> make it figure as part of a story. If it be difficult,
> couple its acquisition with some prospect of
> personal gain.[11]

Oh, and I can't resist philosopher-king Daniel Dennett's description of the brain as a "necktop."

The Transportational Power of Storytelling

In *The Storytelling Book* (2015), I referred to the 'trans' powers of storytelling: to transform, translate and transfix. I want to briefly return to the topic.

Firstly, I want to redefine and even reclaim the 'transportation model.' In the world of communication theory (in which I grew up, professionally speaking), this was the generic term for all those theories that emphasized the linear-sequential view of human decision-making.

AIDA, AIETA and DAGMAR all have at their core a belief that there are various stages of behaviour that 'consumers' (don't start me on that word) go through in making a decision. The idea is that 'consumers' go through a defined sequence, culminating in the marketer's holy grail of purchase.

AIDA stands for 'awareness/attention, interest, desire, action.' Its origins are slightly murky, but they seem to date back to advertising pioneer Elias St Elmo Lewis in the early 20th century.

AIETA stands for 'awareness, interest, evaluation, trial, adoption' and originates with Everett Rogers in 1962.[12]

DAGMAR, developed by Russell H Colley in 1961 is slightly different.[13] His model says that an effective advertising campaign should cause awareness, comprehension, conviction and action (ACCA). However, the idea is better known by its objectives: 'defining advertising goals for measuring advertising results' (DAGMAR).

These theories paved the way for very fact-based, rational advertising campaigns, given that many originated in direct response communications.

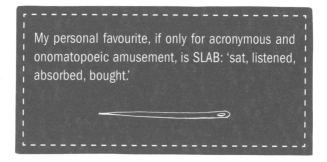

My personal favourite, if only for acronymous and onomatopoeic amusement, is SLAB: 'sat, listened, absorbed, bought.'

Once, these models held firm sway, but rejecting them is no longer heretical. They have been largely discredited by developments in psychology, neuroscience and the recent (tidal) wave of behavioural economics. These emphasize that decisions are more iterative, unconscious, loop-y and context-dependent than the traditional models suggest.

Sadly, though, because they are so linear, rational and safe, these old, decrepit models still offer the veneer of a safety net to some 'advertisers.'

But let's look at the other connotation of 'transport.' The word does not only refer to the humdrum, A-to-B, mind-the-gap-and-ignore-the-information-on-the-dot-matrix-boards of the commuter's existence. It also relates to the feeling of being carried away and transported to other lands, other lives – the sense we get when we are interrupted by arriving at our destination, or when a family member pulls us out of a compelling drama or a crucial football match.

The state of transportation is sometimes described, especially in the world of gaming, as 'immersive.' It is characterized by an "integrative melding of attention, imagery, and feelings, focused on story events."[14]

According to the psychological theory of transportation into narrative worlds, becoming immersed in a story can have powerful emotional and persuasive consequences. The joy of travel and exploration we find from immersion in a story allows our emotions to be engaged and attention to be primed: empathy, absorption and flow all follow. This is why, despite the fact that we know movies featuring sharkna-does or babadooks aren't real, our emotions are deployed as if they were. (This is also why so many psychological experiments use fictional experiences, stories or film clips to study and manipulate real emotions.)

Another paper highlights how the persuasive power of stories has been harnessed to change attitudes and behaviour in various real-world contexts.[15] This paper reported various experiments demonstrating that, when people were told a story, their attitudes shifted in the direction of the story's message. Stories with strong arguments were more persuasive than stories with weak arguments, and, when the level of transportation was high, strong arguments were more persuasive than weak arguments. However, this research also established that even weak arguments included in a story can change attitudes. Thus, stories can persuade (even) in the absence of strong arguments.

Anecdote seems to accord with these findings from academia. Most of what we learn about history, the law, policing, medical matters, politics and the like comes from stories that we read, TV series that we watch and movies that we view. One of the reasons for the popularity of genres like policing or historical fiction is that, for many people, they provide a relatively effortless way of learning about aspects of reality from which we are often shielded.

Here is an essential question for all business presentations. I have always thought that Microsoft's first global campaign – "Where do you want to go to today?" – was a fine example of a big idea that had big goals: to present technology not as enslaving or mystifying, but as liberating and emancipating.

Beware the Narrative Fallacy

Narrative health warning: we can easily fool ourselves with stories that cater to our Platonic thirst for distinct patterns. Similarly, we can be deluded by the narrative fallacy into seeing stories or patterns that are not really there.

In *The Storytelling Book*, I called our brains "pattern-tates" that scan unconsciously for patterns in everything we sense.[16] Just as stories are patterns with meaning, so do our brains edit, select and confabulate by looking for a consistent story or explanation, often in violent disregard of the whole picture.

Journalist Polly Toynbee once said of journalism, "we précis a muddled reality into a narrative of right and wrong." Our love of story means that our brains are in the constant grip of desire for the holistic consistency of a retrospective determinism rather than settling for messy, atomized fragments.[17]

The strength of our storytelling brain – that it constantly wants to fill in the gaps to fabricate a complete story out of disassembled units – can be a dangerous default when it comes to objective analysis of the past and decision-making for the future.

As a result we all – and this is especially the case with the media – find it all too easy to lapse into human-centred narratives, rather than pause for a moment to look for abstract explanations based on social, economic and political factors.

TOP TIPS

1. Remind yourself why we all – and I mean all – love storytelling: why we all watch TV, go to the movies (or used to) and read books (with or without the 'e-'). Imagine how you can use some of that immersive transportation in your work or love life.

2. Imagine you are telling a story on Graham Norton's red chair: what would make the best impression and stop Hugh Jackman or Benedict Cumberbatch pulling the lever? How would you make your document, essay, CV or Tinder profile lever-proof?

3. Imagine you are a lawyer. Start with the best story, not with the evidence (however counter-intuitive that may seem).

4. Think about the art of rhetoric (not too much) and "apply reason to imagination for the better moving of the will."[18]

5. Write out the three things you loved most about:
   a. *That* book
   b. *That* TV programme
   c. *That* film
   d. Maybe even *that* email, tweet or meme
   … and work out how to capture some of it yourself.

6. Ensure that you aren't saying something just because you want it to be said, because you feel it's incredibly fascinating and important, or because it makes you feel good.

7. We can't all be Dean Burnett (limited to one person as things stand), but we can all conjure up a really memorable metaphor for who we are, what we do, what is special about us and what we have to say.

8. Is there a word or image that will transport your audience away from the humdrum and the generic, or enable them to see you or your persuasive power in a new light?

PART 1

STARTING ON THE RIGHT FOOT

We start by addressing the potential problem of being ignored before moving on to how not to get entangled in the weeds of jargon. Then we unveil the six guiding principles of storytelling.

	What you will learn	What you will do	What that will lead to
Week 1: Get Past Attention Spam	How not to be ignored, and not to rely on facts and information	An exercise to ensure you don't get buried in the weeds	Thinking about the virtues of emotions, attention and simplicity
Week 2: Junk the Jargon	To rid your material of as much stale, formal jargon as possible	An exercise that forces you to replace the meaningless with the meaningful	Getting into the right space to apply the SIMPLE principles
Week 3: Be SIMPLE	The six guiding principles of storytelling	Exercises that show the benefits of structure, meaning and memorability	Avoiding ODCAN (one damn chart after the next) and leading towards the importance of structure

GET PAST ATTENTION SPAM

	What you will learn	**What you will do**	**What that will lead to**
Week 1: Get Past Attention Spam	How not to be ignored, and not to rely on facts and information	An exercise to ensure you don't get buried in the weeds	Thinking about the virtues of emotions, attention and simplicity

The first leg of our storytelling journey looks at some theoretical assumptions that underpin how we present, write, argue and persuade. The chief barrier we have to hurdle is that of being ignored. The convention we need to question is that facts and information are the way to grab and retain attention.

So, let's explore some of the often implicit assumptions that have come to dominate the language of presenting and arguing across the various domains we are concerned with.

Let's question how we think communication, speaking and writing work best. Or, if you prefer different terminology, let's examine the epistemology of persuasion. This is about what works and what doesn't.

Then let's eliminate what doesn't, even if it's in vogue and deployed by our bosses, heroes and so-called betters. We may even feel guilty of some form of philosophical insubordination.

And let's look at some of the misplaced theories of science that lead many writers and speakers into the Dungeon of Unintelligibility.

But first, let's examine a couple of metaphors – particularly pernicious ones, too: that the brain is either like a computer or like a sponge.

ATTENTION SPAM

I have previously written about Linda Stone's coinage 'CPA,' or 'continuous partial attention,' and how the brain is designed to work on the basis of energy efficiency and effortlessness rather than seeking perfection, truth or 'what is right.'[19] It is so easy for the brain to act as a filtering device, screening out what it expects to see, has seen before or considers to fall into the category of 'nothing to see here... move along.'

For too long, two metaphors have dominated thinking about the brain, and neither helps in the context of storytelling.

Firstly, the brain as an all-knowing, all-processing computer is the latest in a line of metaphors based on the most advanced technology of the day. These began in the time of Aristotle with the hydraulic system, which was followed by the automaton, then the clock, then the telephone exchange (ask your parents) and now, of course, the computer. The language of 'hard-wired' neural nets and (my least favourite) 'bandwidth' has now been broadly co-opted.

But there are a raft of significant differences between our brain and a computer.

For one thing, our brain is intimately connected to our body: much of the brain's role is to take in sensory information and respond to it. At the time of writing, despite the best efforts of those in Silicon Valley, computers remain disembodied. Computers, of course, lack some of the characteristics of the brain and human discourse. Though there have been some advancements, AI researchers still struggle to imitate certain distinctive human characteristics: emotions, humour, irony and sarcasm (they need more English researchers for the last three). There is also the phenomenon known as the 'uncanny valley' – the weird discomfort we humans feel when we are faced with a robot, AI or digital human. Coined in the 1970s by Masahiro Mori, this term refers to the observation that as robots appear more humanlike, they become more appealing – but only up to a certain point. Then the uncanny valley comes into view, and our affinity is replaced by a sense of creepiness and unease, and a feeling of being in a David Lynch movie. Mori talked about the example of a prosthetic hand.[20]

Secondly, the brain is frequently compared to a sponge.

Again, this is a misleading metaphor. This analogy suggests that our brain is constantly soaking in and absorbing, and by implication retaining everything that it absorbs. Neuroscience suggests otherwise: because the brain accounts for something like 2% of the weight of the average person but needs about 20% of the body's energy, it is on a permanent drive to be as energy efficient as possible. (Much of nature and evolution can be best understood in terms of the drive for efficiency – adapting what is there and avoiding as much redundancy as possible.)

So, in fact, the brain values effortless efficiency more than objective truth. As a result, very often, this effortlessness tends towards the most efficient (or 'satisficing,' in the language of behavioural economics) decision rather than the best.

Therefore, we need to rid ourselves of the sponge metaphor too, as it can seduce us into believing that our audience/reader/potential employer/person-whose-eyes-we-want-to-gaze-into-longingly-forever will have unlimited space and time in their brain to voraciously drink in whatever we have to offer.

Instead, it is best to think of the brain as a filtering machine, designed not to soak up but to screen out and ignore incoming messages and information.

Being a big fan of the creative impulse of serendipity (as I discussed in my *The Inspiratorium*[21]), I am delighted to have accidentally created a term for this. One of the myriad occasions I have avoided the services of spellcheck, I was preparing a presentation on attention for a conference. At one point, I spotted that instead of writing the more expected 'attention span,' I had typed 'attention spam.'

> Perhaps I had been over-indulging in some old *Monty Python* clips.

This seemed to fill a gap and succinctly avoid the need for the previous three or four paragraphs. So, I retrofitted a definition using email as the term of reference. In the same way that a certain type of email often ends up in people's spam folder rather than their inbox, attention spam is filtered out by the brain and is not noticed.

Since I coined this expression, I have been using it to refer to the fact that whatever we produce, write or say must be expressly intended to cut though attention spam. This is essential. Otherwise, it is just so much wasted effort.

Compared to the computer and sponge metaphors, this is surely a more accurate and helpful way of thinking about how we should approach communication in every sense.

TOP TIPS

1. Remove the computer and sponge metaphors from your thinking lexicon. They are not helpful.

2. Remember that the brain is energy efficient: it doesn't want to waste energy and time on what isn't relevant or meaningful.

3. So, unless otherwise informed, always assume you will be filtered out and then develop ways to avoid that fate.

Next, let's move on to the issue of delusory theories of science and how they get in the way of the storytelling apparatus.

THE SCOURGE OF REDUCTIONISM: WALK AWAY, RENÉ

The modern era has, without doubt, seen the ascendancy of science. However, in the business world, this is a particular type of science: one based on physics, reductionism and ruthless standardization. Unless we acknowledge this – and repel or repeal it – we cannot hope to use storytelling in its full panoply. So, now it is time for some history, science and metaphorical archaeology.

In the 17th century, at a time when the machine was fast becoming the dominant icon of the age, the world saw these wondrous new mechanisms as the most elegant way of conceptualizing human endeavour. Inspired by the machines that were beginning to populate the world – from fairground automata to the elaborate clocks decorating churches – people claimed that life could be explained by the same processes of physics and chemistry.

One of the leaders of this movement was the philosopher René Descartes. As well as coining one of the world's most T-shirtable slogans ("I think, therefore I am"), he tried to bring the new mechanistic perspective to bear on the mind/body issue. Along with Galileo, Francis Bacon and others, he established the modern 'analytical' approach, often called the 'scientific method.' Stripped to its bare bones, his method consisted of breaking down big problems into small ones, using the methods of science and mathematics. His real goal was to conquer the inner workings of the human mind. This he endeavoured to do by proposing that the mind and the body were really two different kinds of 'stuff': the body was easily reconcilable with the clockwork motif of the day, whereas the mind or soul was located in a different dimension, only interacting with the body via the pineal gland. This system, known as 'Cartesian dualism,' was intrinsically based on a mathematical approach, and it led to the formulation of sciences for new domains, such as language.

Later, this mechanistic manifesto was made explicit in Julien Offray de La Mettrie's *L'Homme Machine*, published in 1747. This was a full century before the onset of the culture and art that created futurism, modernism and the 'shock of the new.' It was also a full 225 years before Kraftwerk and Gary Numan.

Now, in the realm of science, we have seen the shift from the primacy of physics to the supremacy of biology. This was brutally expressed by no less an authority than James Watson, Nobel Laureate and celebrated co-discoverer of the structure of DNA:

> There is only one science – physics: everything else is social work.[22]

HOW TO SUCCEED
IN BUSHINESS

But biology is plainly not physics. For example, in the case of biology, there are feedback loops at work: the relationships between genes, organisms and environments are reciprocal, and all three are both causes and effects. This contrasts sharply with the linear, escalator-type approach of classical physics, with its emphasis on predictability and consequences.

The metaphor preferred by Darwin himself was not that of the ladder but of the tree. Though still a linear image, it does embrace a far greater degree of complexity by depicting the various branches off the central trunk and including roots in the picture.

But, whereas the Tree of Life could still be viewed as an icon of progress (with species misleadingly shown as 'progressions' or improvements over other species), later commentators emphasized the fact that a far better (for which read 'truer') image was that of the bush. This is because the bush places greater emphasis on the diversity of its branches (species) and far less emphasis on any external notions of progress or directionality. Hence, it is not inevitable that humanity is the endpoint (or, as Aristotle said, the *telos*).

An even more elegant way of putting this fact comes from Steven Rose:

In biology 1+1= 59.[23]

Complexity thinking, a branch of science focussed on holistic and non-linear approaches, has very much responded to the reductionism enterprise by emphasizing the importance of non-linearity, feedback loops, holism and reductionism's tendency to convert a dynamic process into a static phenomenon. The slogan that 'more is different' is well worth heeding.

FREE YOURSELF FROM REDUCTIONISM

So, here are some principles to adhere to before we move on to Week 2:

1. Think of people as people, not atomized reified cogs of standardized homogeneity. Whether this is your audience, your readers, the person interviewing you, your students, your date or your prospective life partner, avoid the reductionism of simplifying everything to the point of meaninglessness.

2. When using data (numbers or facts), bear in mind that the brain does not run on data alone. Avoid cold-hearted calculus if you are dealing with real people (so, for example, why not replace the word 'consumers' with 'people'?).

3. Also if you work with data, do not fear the nightmare of imprecision.

4. The current trend towards a 'tick-box' culture means that Big Data and algorithms are creeping ever deeper into all facets of our lives. This means that it is effortless to pigeon-hole and compartmentalize, and we should be alert to the threat. Tick-boxing means that it is very easy to succumb to the lure of speaking, writing or persuading in a manner that falls into the standardized, dehumanized, mechanistic and over-simplified culture of what I call 'arithmocracy':

a system that is unduly obsessed with numbers, metrics and rationalizations.

5. When charts, words, proposals, speeches and lectures are drained of complexity, ambiguity and subtlety, they become meaningless. Human beings thrive on emotion, meaning and story: there is no excuse for scrimping on any of these.

6. Stick this on your wall, fridge, laptop or child: "Statistics are people with the tears dried off."[24]

WEEK 1

Exercise

Here is your exercise to start putting into practice everything you've learned in Week 1:

Choose a topic – presentation, CV, Tinder profile – and start by clearing the decks and examining some assumptions.

	Am I assuming I have an audience of sponges?	What do my audience not know or not want to hear?	What must I take out?	What can I do to make my words more human?
1				
2				
3				

WEEK 2
JUNK THE JARGON

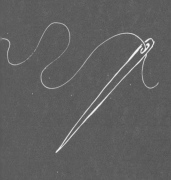

	What you will learn	**What you will do**	**What that will lead to**
Week 2: Junk the Jargon	To rid your material of as much stale, formal jargon as possible	An exercise that forces you to replace the meaningless with the meaningful	Getting into the right space to apply the SIMPLE principles

JARGON IS A CLOAK
TO HIDE BEHIND
THE FACT YOU HAVE
NOTHING NEW OR
MEANINGFUL TO SAY.

This week, in order to build the foundations, we need to appreciate the extent to which jargon is an obstacle to storytelling and remove as much of it as possible.

Let's begin with some detoxing-cum-cathartic de-standard-ization. There is no better place to start than by addressing the issues of jargon and cliché head-on.

Why? Because for all the prevalence of (and secret affection for) jargon, it has a crushing and stultifying effect on our ability to tell stories.

This also means trying to be distinctive, meaningful and appealing on job sites, in CVs and on LinkedIn pages. Take these examples from that very site, which I dredged up from a superficial trawl (names have been removed to protect the jargonized):

> A young, enthusiastic professional looking to climb to the top of the ladder. Succeeds through a creative approach, which is aware of the bigger picture, generating pragmatic solutions that deliver results.

And:

> Service oriented commercial specialist implementing early adoption strategies to meet customer demand & exceed expectations.

When I'm lecturing or guiding students and young people who are applying for jobs, this kind of thing is precisely what I exhort them to avoid: a list of generic 'product benefits' loosely assembled from the IKEA career catalogue with nothing remotely in the vicinity of a feeling that could be mistaken for human, differentiated or evocative. It also doesn't help that the second one appears to have been translated from Hungarian into English via Swedish by a disinterested Russian bot.

A prospective employer (another occasional hat of mine) will find it all too easy to unthinkingly put such statements into the 'ignore' or 'reject' pile. As we have seen (see Week 1), 'attention spam' means that the brain notices what is different and screens out what is to be expected.

Jargon is not always inappropriate or inane: much of it operates as a bonding mechanism amongst group members as a way of cherishing and reinforcing their otherness. Some can be found in the domains of lawyers, accountants and the like. And some is a method of validating fee structures... But, even when jargon is a shared language amongst an in-group, it can still leak outside, where it looks like the ramblings of a deranged AI.

Much like in the BBC TV spoof series *W1A* (2014–2017), where we saw a 'Director of Better,' we now have a plethora of people happy to take on the mantle of 'Head of Agile.' I am sorely tempted to set up a company called Cabbage so I can appoint a 'Head of Cabbage' (or even a company called Steam for that matter).

> Howard Head, the eponymous founder of the sports equipment company, presumably had 'Head of Head' on his business card.

This may seem like a trivial matter, and some of these self-aggrandizing epithets may indeed simply seem amusingly perverse. However, when they infiltrate a company and dominate communications, something vital is drained away. I therefore believe that the weaponization of jargon is more than just a trifle to be dismissed out of hand.

But how dangerous can it be, you might ask?

Jargon remains the bane of our professional lives. It reduces and dehumanizes, and it debases and brutalizes meaning (that's why I like to call it 'de-meaning'). Yet we are besieged by it.

It creates tribes and cliques of jargonauts who aren't adventurers navigating an odyssey of discovery but introverted priests guarding their own interest. To paraphrase Bertrand Russell, they want certainty, not knowledge. This is just one aspect of the reductionist, Taylorist arithmocracy that has been introduced via management consultants and is now seeping its way into the pores of so many aspects of our lives.

The search for safety and predictability, the obsession with rationality and logic (call it System 2 thinking if you want[25]), well, it takes the joy out of working with people. We might joke about the clichés and the corporate book of acronyms thrust into the clammy hands of inductees (I can name names here), but we cannot have a true storytelling culture if the baggage of jargon is still on the communication carousel.

Two recent examples stand out for me from the world of communications. Marcus is an online lending service from Goldman Sachs that is named after the company's founder, Marcus Goldman. It launched its campaign in 2019 with the slogan "You Can Money." It aimed to be simple and straightforward, and to encourage people to be at ease with money (all noble objectives for any financial institution), but the verbing still grates.

Next in the dock is the Aperol spritz, an aperitif named after the Italian slang word *apero* ('open'). It recently started a campaign with the strapline "Together We Joy." Ad agency JWT Milan promised to create something for the brand that would "give it a new way of expressing itself and of talking to people... exactly as Aperol manages to intercept everyone's tastes."[26] Clearly, it chose to use verbing as its approach.

Now, any grammar maven will tell you that language is constantly evolving and that verbing goes back at least as far as Shakespeare, who is known as a prolific neologizer.

However, beyond the mockery, communication depends on some simple, unarguable principles: jargon and clichés should be shut down rather than given free rein. Jargon immunizes us against the messy, emotional complexity of human behaviour and it turns our company cultures, our lives and our relationships into drains, not radiators.

So, can't we all ditch the stilted legalese, officialese and McKinseyese, avoid the semantic ping-pong as far as possible, and actually agree on the basics of human interaction: what do these words *mean*?

WEEK 2

Exercise

Now let's start putting these ideas into practice:

1. Start by looking at your company website, your internal or external communications, your CV or your dating profile (column 1).

2. Identify all the words, expressions and acronyms that are generic or clichéd husks of meaning, or where, if you're being honest, you don't actually understand them (column 2).

3. Replace as many of these words, expressions and acronyms as you can with something simple, human, full of meaning and universally understood (column 3).

I've completed the first line for you as an example.

Location	Meaningless words and phrases	Replacement words and phrases
Homepage	*My company homepage talks about how as a company "we offer a holistic approach to solutionizing."*	*"We know our customers have a wide range of problems. We have the experience and expertise to help solve them."*

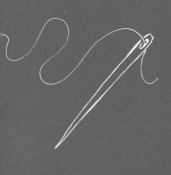

WEEK 3
BE SIMPLE

	What you will learn	**What you will do**	**What that will lead to**
Week 3: Be SIMPLE	The six guiding principles of storytelling	An exercise that shows the benefits of structure, meaning and memorability	Avoiding ODCAN (one damn chart after the next) and leading towards the importance of structure

So far, we have identified – and hopefully addressed – the problem of attention spam, then removed the meaningless debris of junk. Let's move on and establish some guiding principles for our storytelling journey.

The letters of the word SIMPLE form a, well, simple acronym-mnemonic (an acromnemonic?!).

1. **S**trictly **S**tructured
2. **I**nsightfully **I**nspiring
3. **M**emorably **M**eaningful
4. **P**ersuasive **P**oint of View
5. **L**anguage-**L**ed
6. **E**motionally **E**mpathetic

STRICTLY STRUCTURED

Story relies on structure – not just plot, message or characters, but structure. Probably the most prevalent fault I see in material of all sorts (documents, students' essays, presentations and so on) is an absence of structure.

Someone once said, "History is just one damned thing after another."[27] To paraphrase this insight, too often what we write and present is one damn fact – or one damn slide – after another.

So, how can we avoid ODCAN, or one damn chart after the next?

INSIGHTFULLY INSPIRING

In *The Inspiratorium*, I explored the value and sources of insight in the business of brands and marketing.[28] The transformative power of insight lies in its ability to change your viewpoint and perspective, whether you are working with a brand that wants to be repositioned, a policy that needs to be reframed, or a person seeking a new outlook or personality.

Often when I work with commercial clients or even with my students, it becomes clear that what they have produced does in fact contain an insight: something that makes me see their business, their brand, their analysis or their personality in a new light.

But often it is buried away in a forest of detail – a needle of illumination in a haystack of gloom.

These insights, when they can be identified, can often be inspiring (the other 'i'). And what is the goal of our speeches, our papers and our words if not to inspire a response or reaction in our audience?

Etymologically, the word 'inspire' – like 'respiratory' and 'spirit' – has its roots in words meaning 'blowing' or 'breathing upon' or 'infusing'.

We take this for granted too often. Instead, always ask yourself: what emotion or action am I trying to generate here, and how can I achieve that?

MEMORABLY MEANINGFUL

Stories are so effective across all cultures, religions, faiths and ages for a number of reasons, one of which is the fact that they create and reinforce memories. Think how many stories you heard as a child, and how many you have passed on to your own children or grandchildren (or other people's).

Then think about why this is such a crucial cultural phenomenon. The reason is that stories embody learning and wisdom.

When I carry out my training sessions, I invite attendees to bring a story with them to share with the group. We then listen to, absorb and learn from each story.

This is proof of the power of the stories we hear as children to stir us, direct us, educate us and move us: precisely the values we seek when we become parents ourselves.

They become part of the structure of our memory, always alive and always ready to be reignited in the right context and with the right audience. Memories are intrinsic to who we are, and stories are the key vehicles for those memories.

We retain memories with such attachment because they are *meaningful* to us. As we touched upon in Week 2, human beings thrive on the meaningful: what does something mean to us, and how does it affect, move, and inspire create and emotion in us? One of the goals of the creative arts is to build meaning for us, to explain the world or show it in a new light.

Try to ensure that whatever you are writing, saying or creating is meaningful. This will make it memorable.

PERSUASIVE POINT OF VIEW

Next in line is something that should feel unarguable but may need reiterating. Since the classical rhetoricians and speakers – such as Aristotle, Quintilian and Cicero – the study of the art of persuasion has been paramount for anyone in the public arena.

If you are not committed to persuasion in what you are declaiming, what are you doing at all?

But remember, 'persuasion' is not a synonym for 'showing lots of facts.' Persuasion does not just mean the naked transmission of information from sender to receiver. One of the oldest – and simplest – theories of communication suggests that before any useful outcome can be achieved from a communication, the receiver has to accurately understand the sender's idea. This means the message has to be effective in the receiver's space. If the message does not grip the receiver, the sender is wasting their time. The encoding of the message is the creation of the message, and communication therefore is best seen as a system of coded meanings. In the communication process, the communicator/encoder has to give shape to the message. The encoder encodes the message rightly in their mind and transmits it to the receiver; then, the receiver interprets and decodes the message according to their experience and understanding.

Another important concept to keep in mind is point of view. Eagle-eyed readers may have spotted that my company name is POV, so a little personal anecdote now follows.

Some 20 years ago, I wanted to leave the five-day-a-week treadmill not just because I wanted to downshift but also because I wanted to test my capacities and faculties in new ways. I had grown to fancy the idea of doing training and development, wanted to deepen my involvement with the Phoenix Cinema (the oldest continually working cinema in the UK) and wanted to try out what Charles Handy called a "portfolio life."[29]

So, I gave it a go without any specific compartmentalization. But I did feel the need for some sort of branding (Tas was pretty good for existing loyal users but maybe too vague for prospects). The name I chose for the company fell out of two of my interests.

My ad agency existence had brought me moderately close to the end (creative) product, and involvement with the 'creative work' had always been one of my favoured heartlands. I remembered seeing many scripts, too, that used a particular convention of screenwriting: when describing what we would see on screen, the term 'POV' would often be used to recount what would be seen from the 'point of view' of a particular character. It was also apparent that a point of view has a particular and more strategic meaning: the espousal of an opinion, belief system, perspective or angle that gives its owner a singular vantage point on the world.

So, if what you are communicating has no POV but is merely a bare, dusty transmission of facts, why bother to communicate at all?

(I accept that there are some circumstances – for example, when writing about government and public policy – where absolute neutrality is required and facts are to be presented without any interpretation. But I think such situations are rarer than is often thought. And, even then, the person with the data should be allowed or encouraged to present points of view or hypotheses that emerge.)

LANGUAGE-LED

No friend of jargon or cliché am I, as we have seen (see Week 2). Not only is it essential to weed the garden of mind-numbing jargon and clear out the clichés, but we must also look more positively at how we express ourselves.

Let's begin with the word 'content.' There is nothing wrong with it of itself (it is not too complicated or twaddle-ish), but it does have a rather over-flattering view of itself. Clients are wont to talk of 'content strategy' and 'content management,' but at heart 'content' is just 'stuff' with better PR. And there is good stuff and bad stuff.

Calling what you have to say (whether in your dating profile or your company's homepage) 'content' does not make it inherently more interesting to your audience. And if clients say "I really need to put content on Twitter" I delicately suggest this might be something they might want to think about before irretrievably pushing any buttons.

The next stage after ridding ourselves, our colleagues and our culture of the scourge of jargon is to attempt to set the bar higher in terms of the language we use across all media. This applies to our documents, our presentations and our CVs, and maybe even to the barrage of emails we send and receive on a nano-second basis.

In short, many of us have achieved reasonable levels of literacy. Many will have gone on to further education. Many more – ideally more – of us read books and other sources of literature. So, there is surely no reason why we can't all try to elevate the level of linguistic ingenuity and diversity that we bring to our communication.

Words like 'revolutionary', 'visionary' and 'game-changing' have become clichéd and risk over-promising. Then there is the plethora of websites and advisers offering untold wealth if we just use words like 'free', 'new' or 'act now'.

One of my least favourite words – one I try to avoid at all costs – is 'passionate'. Apart from being overused, is it really apposite for your brand, your website or your personality? Consider too whether it makes you sound generic – how many other people, brands and services will you be competing with who claim to be similarly 'passionate'?

At least explore the possibility of other expressions – synonyms that show you have made the effort to be different or sound different from your competitors.

WEEK 3

Exercise 1

Consider replacing "I am/we are/the brand is passionate about" with something more original – with your own colour, tone of voice and personality.

Take 30 minutes and come up with three different ways of writing it in your own style.

1

2

3

Now here are some I made earlier:

1.   I am intensely interested in...

2.   I really appreciate...

3.   I have an ardent/vivid desire for...

4.   I am avid/eager/zealous about...

5.   I love being engrossed in...

6.	I find myself utterly absorbed/stirred/roused/rapt by...
7.	I am nothing short of fanatical about...
8.	I have always been enthusiastic about...
9.	I have devoted much of my time to...
10.	I get excited/animated about...
11.	I am enthralled/fascinated by...
12.	I think I may have the gene for...
13.	Nothing gets me more excited than...
14.	I find... irresistible
15.	I am a very curious person *(depending on the audience and context.)* Or, my curiosity has always been piqued by...
16.	I am perpetually dazzled by...
17.	I have always treasured...
18.	I have always been struck by...
19.	I am thrilled to...
20.	There is nothing I like more than to wallow in...

And try and do this whenever you are tempted to use some debased and generic expression.

The best use of language doesn't always contain the fewest words. Rather than using one word that is dangerously clichéd and bereft of meaning, why not let your brain have a little fun and extend your linguistic prowess to increase your chances of being memorably meaningful?

EMOTIONALLY EMPATHETIC

The last letter contains two more *sine qua nons* of storytelling that are emphatically important to all forms of communication.

There are plenty of testaments to the importance of the behavioural economics enterprise in my previous books. However, as a trainer and lecturer in that domain, I can't let go of the chance to throw further light on the need to address emotions in all our communications.

Francis Bacon believed that the duty of rhetoric is "to apply reason to imagination for the better moving of the will," as he said in *"Of The Proficience and Advancement of Learning"* in 1605. He said that the basic job requirement of a rhetorician is to discover and apply the best available means of persuasion. One of Aristotle's insights which preceded Bacon was that this could only happen if pathos (emotion or feeling) was triggered.

Most of us never get to be anyone like Diana Prince, a boy wizard, Holden Caulfield, Jon Snow, Ted Hastings or Offred, but stories transport us into a world where we can put ourselves in their shoes, hearts and minds (see the Prologue for more on transportation). We can face their moral dilemmas, we can feel their passions, and we can imagine how we would act in their place.

Empathy, rightly and finally, is enjoying some time in the spotlight at the moment. We are realizing how much better human beings we can be if we move away from our confirmation biases and echo chambers and force ourselves to empathize with those we would not normally consort with.

Storytelling is the original empathy-generation machine. What better way to learn about other people, cultures or worlds (and indeed ourselves) than through the miraculous transportation of story?

BONUS:
EFFECTIVENESS AND EFFICIENCY

Let me stress one other proposition.

I hope that everything you find in this book – and everything you work on as you read it and subsequently put into practice – will make you a more effective persuader, presenter, writer, job applicant and date magnet.

But I hope it will make you more efficient, too.

By this, I mean that I believe that following these principles and practices should help you to waste less time by:

- Ensuring that you spend less time preparing speeches, decks, emails and comments that go into people's attention spam never to re-emerge
- Wasting less time giving those talks and presentations (which, sad but true, no one cares about – soz)
- Writing less (i.e. writing more efficiently) so meetings can be shorter and/or partially eliminated

Some of these require broader organizational or cultural change. However, I have worked with several organizations that have implemented these ideas and reduced wastage while improving their persuasiveness and focus.

One final reminder.

I like to think that no one in the history of humanity has ever uttered the following sentence:

I wish that presentation had been longer.

WEEK 3

Exercise 2

Let's take a step back and look at the six principles, before putting them into practice:

	What do I do to have a clear Structure, avoiding ODCAN?	Do I have an Insight?	What is the idea, image or picture that will be Memorable and Meaningful to my audience?	How am I being Persuasive (emotionally, not just factually)?	Is my Language human, articulate and clear?	How can I create Emotion and Empathy in my audience?
1						
2						
3						

PART 2

GETTING TO THE HEART OF THE MATTER

We have now established the fundamental building blocks over the first three weeks. The middle third of this workbook is where we start to introduce and build the next storey (story?) of a storytelling approach.

	What you will learn	What you will do	What that will lead to
Week 4: Weave a Golden Thread	The power of structure and framework	An exercise where you weave your own thread	Having the essential components of storytelling in place
Week 5: Create Conflict	Why you can't have a real story without conflict	An exercise where you design conflict into your document, CV, profile etc.	Being ready to bring in one key emotion
Week 6: Surprise!	Why surprise will help us evade attention spam	An exercise where you inject surprise and witness the results	Preparing for the last three ingredients

WEEK 4

WEAVE
A GOLDEN
THREAD

	What you will learn	**What you will do**	**What that will lead to**
Week 4: Weave a Golden Thread	The power of structure and framework	An exercise where you weave your own thread	Having the essential components of storytelling in place

"A STORY IS A PATH
THROUGH THE WOOD."

PHILIP PULLMAN
(ATTRIBUTED)

I wrote in *The Storytelling Book* about the central importance of what I call the 'golden thread.'[30] The idea is rooted in the myth of Theseus and the Minotaur, where Ariadne gives Theseus a ball of golden thread to help him navigate his way through the maze that is the labyrinth, so he can find the Minotaur, slay him and safely find his way out.

The idea of the guiding thread – powerful but subtle – has always seemed to me an apposite metaphor for structure, framework and guidance in everything that we write and present. Think of it, if you like, as creating order from (potential) chaos. We might call the extra bits that we discard 'exformation', a term coined by Danish science writer, Tor Norretranders.

This is in line with the findings of neuroscience. Our brain finds it so much easier to follow a thread or line. Once it has grasped the thread, the brain retains it.

The evidence suggests that our brain tends to avoid the problems of clutter by retaining the gist of what it has seen or heard but gleefully discarding the details. So, although we can retain deep structure (the meaning and sense of what was said) for long periods of time, we can only accurately remember surface structure (the words that were used) for around eight to ten seconds.

So, think of the golden thread as what you want to leave your audience with: the words, images, metaphors or feelings that you are seeking to impress on them. But this will only work if it is part of a structured strand of argument.

On the subject of weaving as a metaphor for narration, we often talk of 'spinning a yarn,' and those who advise politicians on how to frame their stories are labelled 'spin doctors' (amongst other more judgemental and less delicate terms). Many fairy tales involve spinning – think *Sleeping Beauty* or *Rumpelstiltskin*, and also the Czech fairy tale *The Golden Spinning Wheel* or the Scottish folk tale *Habitrot*.

In the world of the movies, we can do worse than listen to Andrew Stanton. Even if you haven't heard of him, you've almost certainly seen some of the movies he has written, co-written and/or directed for Pixar. These include *Monsters Inc.* (2001), *Finding Nemo* (2003), *Wall-E* (2008), *Finding Dory* (2016) and all four *Toy Story* films.

In a justly celebrated TED Talk in 2012, Stanton gave his own take on the key to memorable storytelling:

> I first started really understanding this storytelling device when I was writing with Bob Peterson on *Finding Nemo*... **It's the invisible application that holds our attention to story.** I don't mean to make it sound like this is an actual exact science, it's not. That's what's so special about stories, they're not a widget, they aren't exact. Stories are inevitable, if they're good, but they're not predictable.[31]

Similarly, the poet Wayne Koestenbaum calls this process "organizing lava."[32] This is another vivid metaphor akin to the golden thread. Lava is a destructive force of nature that can sweep away everything in its wake, and too often we are the lava and let it wreak its havoc with everything that comes into its path. Organizing lava (the deliberately oxymoronic feel is surely deliberate) is your goal.

Another popular analogy that writers are wont to parade is the 'path through the woods.' Philip Pullman, creator of the *Northern Lights* universe, wrote in one of his essays that the storyteller's duty is to the path and not the woods, and a path is always a path *to*: it needs a destination.[33] A path is also a choice – a forking of options (think of Robert Frost's 1916 poem "The Road Not Taken," about a young man hiking through a forest who is abruptly confronted with a fork in the path).

WEEK 4

Exercise 1

Let's try an exercise with your deck, CV, Tinder profile or anything else:

	The logic and flow of my argument is...	What gets in the way as 'exformation' is...	Chart by chart, line by line, is this true but useless?
1			
2			
3			

STORYBOARDING YOUR GOLDEN THREAD

How do you devise and develop your golden thread? Storyboard it.

A technique that has long been used in the movie business and in the ad world, storyboarding is now used anywhere film is shot (even commonly for marketing and sales videos). It is an important part of the commercial pre-production process because it clearly conveys how the story will flow shot by shot, image by image. You can see how your shots work together along the overall thread. It also allows you to see any problems that might go unnoticed, ultimately saving you time and money. It is a roadmap, a journey, the visual depiction of the path through the woods.

The benefits are manifold.

One of the chief reasons to use storyboards is that doing so allows everyone who has a stake in the production to visualize what is in the mind of the director and the writer. This makes it easier for everyone involved to imagine the same thing and get closer to achieving buy-in from the team.

With a film, there is a benefit of expediency too: making changes to a few frames on a board is immeasurably cheaper than having to alter something once it's been shot. Similarly, in ad agencies, storyboards provide a bridge between what creatives (and a director) might envisage and what the client has expected in their finished 30-second TV ad, with all the concomitant savings of doing it in advance and shooting on paper, not on film.

TOP TIPS

1. This is not about the detail. Let me say that again, but with feeling. *This is not about the detail*.

2. Unlike in a movie, you don't need to worry about scope, frame, setting or characters. However, there is one very clear analogy that holds: the storyboard shows what your angle, point of view or thread is focused on. David Mamet once declared that one of the main questions a director must answer is, "Where do I put the camera?"[34] Hence, your storyboard is your point of view, your angle, your focus.

3. One term that is shared by film directors and members of the Worshipful Clan of Behavioural Economics is the word 'framing.' For the Spielbergs and Tarantinos, framing is how you shoot a scene, the angle and the marking. But, outside Tinseltown, framing involves taking logically equivalent information and presenting it in a different light. For example, saying that 90% of patients will survive for five years after taking a particular medical treatment is factually identical to saying that 10% will die. However, the two pieces of information are not processed by the brain in the same way. Assuming that your goal is to persuade somebody to take a treatment, the first frame will be more effective.

4. Clearly, there is never one definitive, canonical point of view. The advantage of developing a thread and storyboarding is precisely so you can play with different threads and see which ones are more tantalizing and surprising, or more unexpected. You can examine how they position you or your brand as the 'hero', and consider which is truer to the data and information you might be showing. The beauty of the storyboard is that it is a perfect bridge between thinking randomly about different options at one end, and committing to the final draft (or, worse still, the vomit draft) at the other end.

5. Storyboarding is also a great time-saver. Week 3 talked about the need to enhance efficiency, and a storyboard has the simple benefit of being easy to change. This is all the more straightforward if (like me) you use sticky notes. They are cheap, easy to use and then discard, and have the not insignificant benefit of being movable. This is really important as it allows you – even encourages you – to play around with your thread until you feel comfortable with what you have.

TOP TIPS

6. At the heart of the storyboarding exercise will be the drive to find one or more threads that will achieve your goal. Needless to say, that goal will depend on your circumstances and context – for example, whether you are trying to present a chunk of data to a marketing director, write a speech for Year 8 parents, or impress a potential employer or love interest. Take your material and work out as many threads as you can, each with their own argument, slant or angle.

7. How do you know when you have the right thread? Well, teamwork is one answer. If you are already in a work environment where the team dynamic is supportive, develop your thread with your colleagues. Or show it to someone who isn't part of your team (such as a member of your family) or is working on this specific topic – see how they react to the threads you are proposing. Which do they grasp simply, intuitively and emotionally? Which best marries their response to your goal? Does their reaction suggest a new thread? Similarly, if you're preparing for a job interview or a date, find a friend or a sympathetic parent or sibling (if that's not an oxymoron) as a source of feedback.

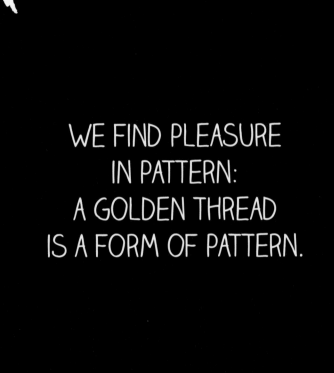

WE FIND PLEASURE
IN PATTERN:
A GOLDEN THREAD
IS A FORM OF PATTERN.

WEEK 4

Exercise 2

Now have a go at designing your own storyboard.

1. Take a bunch of individual sticky notes.

2. On each one, write a logical step, argument or point that you want to make – don't include *any* data or information

3. Make sure that each note links simply to the next

4. When you have the complete thread, stand back

5. Is it clean, clear and consistent?

6. Can you create alternative threads?

7. Which thread seems the most motivating, distinctive and memorable?

CREATE
CONFLICT

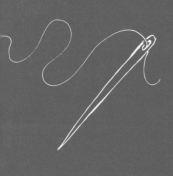

	What you will learn	What you will do	What that will lead to
Week 5: Create Conflict	Why you can't have a real story without conflict	An exercise where you design conflict into your document, CV, profile etc.	Being ready to bring in one key emotion

When I think of all the decks I see, the essays I (have to) read, and the presentations and speeches I (often, also have to) watch, it is painfully apparent why they are generally so memorably forgettable and unaffecting.

There is no conflict.

The secret to storytelling – and one that was known by our first ancestral weavers of tales – is that we need a conflict, a struggle, an argument, a disagreement, a problem or a polarity for the brain to get involved. It forces us to ponder and cogitate at the rational level, but also at the more emotional level it gets us invested – it makes us *take sides.* As we saw with our SIMPLE principles (see Week 3), story is rooted in empathy.

Conflict piques our curiosity and encourages us to ask: Why are these two forces at odds? How will the conflict play out? Who will win? How will victory affect them (and us)? What will happen to the loser? And what would I do if I were in that situation?

The essence of all drama is conflict: how individuals deal with conflict shows us the kind of person they are. It also gives us lessons to learn from.

Building inner tension that is morally complex is universally gripping. As Kurt Vonnegut said:

> Somebody gets into trouble and gets out of it again. People *love* that story. They *never* get sick of it.[35]

Conflict arises from a situation or meeting between characters that results in challenge and opposition. Conflict – for example, a power struggle between a hero (or protagonist) and a villain (or antagonist) – is arguably the key element in fiction, because without conflict there is no movement and no narrative drive. Conflict challenges a character's convictions and values, and highlights their strengths, motivations, values and/or weaknesses, much as it does in real life. Conflict forces characters to reveal their real selves (often to themselves).

Conflict tests and proves character in the furnace of strife, by providing barriers and obstacles to be faced and overcome, and generating narrative propulsion. Just to take one instance, in Shakespeare's *Julius Caesar*, Brutus constantly struggles with his feelings towards his friend Caesar and his country.

And conflict is part of life, everyone's life, all the time. This is so for people who are part of an in-group at odds with an out-group, within the family, or even between what Daniel Kahneman popularized as the two thinking processes of System 1 and System 2.[36]

The best way to create something that you think might justify the term 'story' is to build in a conflict from the very start. As David Eagleman said:

> Just like a good drama the human brain runs on conflict.[37]

Or, for those who like their insights wrapped in an equation, try this:

$$CONFLICT = CHARACTER + WANT + OBSTACLE$$

There are always two sides to a conflict, and the resolution of a conflict brings about change and positivity. As storytellers, we must identify and create empathy with both sides of the conflict.

Theorists disagree (you might say they have conflicting opinions), but broadly speaking they have identified six types of conflict. Often a story can contain more than one form of conflict: take *Les Misérables*, where Jean Valjean is in almost constant conflict with his peers, his society, himself and at least one other person (Javert). One central conflict is about the nature of justice and mercy.

As the filmmaker David Lynch said on "The Talks" website:

> Stories hold conflict and contrast, highs and lows, life and death, and the human struggle and all kinds of things.[38]

John le Carré once gave an interview in the *New York Times* in which he explained how storytelling works. This is a beautiful illustration of how story is fuelled by conflict:

> "The cat sat on the mat" is not a story. "The cat sat on the dog's mat" *is* a story.[39]

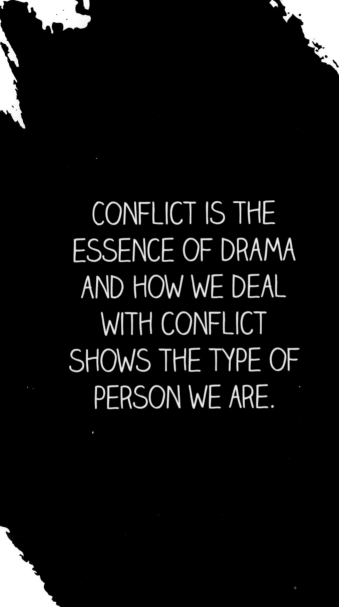

CONFLICT IS THE
ESSENCE OF DRAMA
AND HOW WE DEAL
WITH CONFLICT
SHOWS THE TYPE OF
PERSON WE ARE.

TYPES OF CONFLICT

Let's take a brief look at the six types.

Person vs Self

This is about a psychological struggle within the mind of a character, the resolution of which creates the plot's suspense. Flaws and internal struggles make characters more lifelike and sympathetic.

The conflict happens *within* them, and it drives their development as a character. As James Frey demonstrates in *How to Write a Damn Good Novel* (1987), internal conflicts make characters both interesting and memorable. Intense conflicts and inner strife create the deepest empathy with an audience: we feel their struggles, their torments, their debates, their reluctance. A tortured soul is so much more compelling. Otherwise, a character risks becoming one-dimensional.

Conflicts can work at an emotional, intellectual and/or moral level. A classic example is the *Toy Story* series (having read Week 2, you will understand why I deliberately avoided the word 'franchise' there: a bit too close to jargon for my liking.) Buzz Lightyear embodies the core internal conflict of the movie: he is a toy who doesn't realize he is a toy. As with so many 'inner conflict' stories, what drives the character and makes their struggle so relatable is the gap between who they *think* they are and who they *really* are. It is usually more present within drama, rather than (for example) action or thriller, which will typically be more preoccupied with external conflict.

Fans of *Breaking Bad* (2008–2013) – which has my vote for best TV series *ever* – will be familiar with Walter's struggle between his desire to help his wife and family, on the one hand, and, on the other, his slide into an abyss of crime, which he gradually begins to relish.

Person vs Another Person

This appears in pretty much every story ever written, especially thrillers and mysteries/whodunnits. The *Iliad* has many examples (e.g. Achilles vs Hector and Achilles vs his own leader, Agamemnon). Ask any classicist and they will define the *Iliad* as effectively 'Achilles in a strop'. In *Hamlet*, the eponymous Danish prince is involved in a conflict with his uncle, King Claudius, who wants Hamlet killed. Or Harry and Draco, or Harry and Voldemort. If you've seen Kurt Vonnegut's "Shape of Stories" lecture, you will know of his fascinating insight into why Hamlet is like Cinderella.[40]

All sport embodies this type of conflict, from Roman gladiatorial combat to Federer across the net from Nadal. Oh, and for fans of musicals, there is Alexander Hamilton sparring with Aaron Burr.

Person vs Nature

This is where the hero struggles against primal forces. This may be a survival story or even a fable. Typical topics are weather (*The Perfect Storm*, 2000), animals (*Jaws*, 1975) and natural disasters (*The Day after Tomorrow*, 2004). Take your pick from the Anglo-Saxon epic *Beowulf* to Daniel Defoe's *Robinson Crusoe* (1719) or the films *King Kong* (1933), *The Birds* (1963), *Jurassic Park* (1993), *Titanic* (1997) or *Life of Pi* (2012). Or Herman Melville's novel *Moby Dick* (1851), the story of one man's obsession with overcoming nature (specifically, a whale).

Then there is Jack London's novel *The Call of the Wild* (1903), which features a dog as the main character. The dog has to battle snow, freezing conditions and icy rivers to survive in a new home.

A more modern example is the one that I tend to refer to as "Leonardo DiCaprio vs the bear" (*The Revenant*, 2015). Albert Camus' *La Peste* (1947) is about a plague but also a political allegory (I write this mid-pandemic, to whoever is still out there…). Or, if you can face it, there is Danny Boyle's movie *127 Hours* (2010).

Person vs Society
Here, the struggle against society occurs when a character is at odds with a particular social norm or condition, such as poverty, political partisanship, a social convention, or a particular set of values. The hero's bold and unorthodox (iconoclastic, even) ideas diverge from the norms, customs or practices of tradition. Society ridicules or threatens to ostracize, expel or even eliminate the rebel, compelling them to act. Issues of freedom, justice and morality may

be at stake. This is the home of the maverick, of Romeo and Juliet, of Winston Smith from George Orwell's *Nineteen Eighty-Four* (1949).

For example, in Charles Dickens's *Nicholas Nickleby* (1839), the hero stands against a hypocritical education system, while in *Bleak House* (1852) the antagonist fights a corrupt legal system.

Or take Suzanne Collins's *Hunger Games* trilogy (2008–2010) or Margaret Atwood's *The Handmaid's Tale* (1985). In the former, Katniss Everdeen becomes a symbol of rebellion, just as June/Offred does in Gilead in the latter.

Person vs Technology

The question here is about what it means to be human. Yes, there are commonalities with many other forms of conflict, you may respond, but in this case the distinction is the theme of what sets us apart from machines.

This is the home of (but not exclusively populated by) science fiction. Here we find Mary Shelley's seminal story *Frankenstein* (1818), the story of the first monster created by science; Robert Louis Stevenson's *Strange Case of Dr Jekyll and Mr Hyde* (1886); *Blade Runner* (1982), based on a Philip K Dick novel *Do Androids Dream of Electric Sheep?* (1968); Michael Crichton's *Westworld* (1973) and its TV reboot (2016–); the *Terminator* series (1984–2019); the *Matrix* movies (1999–2021); Alex Garland's *Ex Machina* (2014); and the TV series *Humans* (2015–2018).

The most prominent example is Isaac Asimov's *I, Robot* (1950), which assembled various tales from Asimov. Notable amongst them was "Runaround," where Asimov first introduced the famous Three Laws of Robotics. Much of Asimov's writing (and his legacy) demonstrates conflicts between humans and machines.

Person vs Fate

This is the home of pretty much all Greek tragedy. The *Iliad* and *Odyssey*, to start with, feature men (and often women too) subjected to the whims of the gods, fate or a combination of the two. In the *Odyssey*, Poseidon punishes Odysseus by forcing him to wander from disaster to disaster. Much of Greek epic and tragedy revolves around how humans are subject to the whims of capricious deities.

A rather more modern instance is Elphaba in the novel (1995) and musical (2003–) *Wicked*. She longs to establish her own identity but has to accept her fate as the Wicked Witch of the West.

Person vs the Supernatural

Homer's *Odyssey* abounds in magical creatures and encounters, from the one-eyed Cyclops, Polyphemus, to Circe, the witch who turns Odysseus' sailors into pigs. In more contemporary settings, we have *The Woman in White* (1859), *The Exorcist* (1973), the lighter touch of *Ghostbusters* (1984) and the various iterations of *Dracula*. Almost the whole oeuvre of Stephen King fits under this heading – for example, how the haunted Overlook Hotel drives Jack Torrance to insanity in *The Shining* (1977).

Much of Harry Potter, being about wizardry, operates in this realm too.

Person vs the Unknown

There is some overlap here with other domains, but we can place in this box everything from Wells's *War of the Worlds* (1897) to Steven Spielberg's *Close Encounters of the Third Kind* (1977) and *E.T.* (1982) to Robert Zemeckis's *Contact* (1997), Denis Villeneuve's *Arrival* (2016) and the story of Mark Watney vs Mars in *The Martian* (book, 2011, movie, 2015). And finally, Adam McKay's *Don't Look Up* (2021), a satirical allegory about a comet that will imminently destroy Earth, became one of the most talked about movies of 2021–early 2022.

TOP TIPS

Here are some guidelines about how to create conflict. We will follow this up in the Hero and Villain exercise below.

1. What are the character's key desires – conscious and/or unconscious?

2. How will they face the conflict? Who will they face it with? What people, institutions or forces will line up alongside them or be ranged against them?

3. What is at stake? Every story must have something that will happen if the character fails in their quest, life, hopes or goals.

4. What character traits will they bring to the conflict to ensure they prevail? Are these inherent traits or are they going against the grain?

If you are searching for ways to use conflict in materials designed to influence (such as presentations and documents), here are some suggestions to think about based on what I do myself:

1. Is there conflict between what you were asked to look at (e.g. in research or data analysis) and what you actually found?

2. Is there conflict between members of your audience? Often there will be contradictory expectations and positions espoused by your audience, or by members of your organization. Consider addressing these explicitly.

3. Might your story be even stronger if you expressly highlight the conflict (differences) between one 'consumer' (or opinion) and others that you have identified but rejected?

4. How does this all affect your brand and communications targeting? What may need to be changed?

WEEK 5

Exercise 1

The goal of this exercise is to establish the framework for a story that takes something intrinsically dry and creates something that Martin Amis might describe as having "freshness, energy and reverberation of voice."[41]

This exercise ensures that you have something human and emotional. This will always trump messaging and can help to humanize any issue, brand or challenge. It will also give you a golden thread (see Week 4) – perhaps a metaphor, analogy or 'what if' on which you can hang the rest of your presentation, document, CV or love letter to yourself.

When I use this exercise in my training workshops, we do it in teams so there is a healthy debate. So, feel free to try this out with team members, colleagues, and/or friends and family.

1. TOPIC, ISSUE OR PROBLEM

Choose your topic, your issue or your problem. It can be anything from a brand challenge to a topic for a speech, or a blank piece of paper titled "why you should hire/ spend the rest of your life with me."

2. STRUCTURE AND ARCHETYPES

Next, think about your structure. The structure of a story depends on creating what Carl Jung called "universal archetypes."[42] These are ancient patterns at the heart of storytelling that our ancestors used to help them understand the world and their place in it, and to conceptualize their complex existence in order to learn how to develop patterns of behaviour that would help them to survive and thrive.

According to Jung, our collective unconscious consists of psychic structures and cognitive categories. These are manifested in symbolic imagery and they mould how we look at the world. This accounts for the similarity of so many of our stories and myths ("a sameness of experience," in Jung's words[43]). You can also think of them as collective characters in the cultural unconscious. They seem to occur across geographical and chronological distance.

These basic characters (or types) are ones we find in ancient myths or fairy tales. They continually recur in stories, literature and film, and across all media and channels. They represent basic elements of the human condition that are present in the psyches of all humans.

Archetypes build a relationship that goes beyond the ordinary. They relate to the deepest emotional and unconscious parts of ourselves, and allow expression and understanding of emotion. Writers tend to see them as blank templates that they can imbue with characterization, plot and conflict.

There are, naturally, disagreements as to how many archetypes there are, but they include Everyman, Innocent, Warrior, Child, Creator, Joker/Trickster, Rebel, Ruler, Herald, Guardian and Shadow. Many of these are explored in depth in Christopher Vogler's *The Writer's Journey* (1992). More niche archetypes that recur in myth and legend include magical beasts that turn people into stone. These should be distinguished from fantastical beasts (and where to find them).

In what follows, for simplicity's sake we will concentrate on the three keys archetypes: Hero, Villain and Mentor.

3. CONFLICT

Talk about the topic at hand and find a conflict. Around this conflict, you should find your Hero and Villain. There is no story without a Hero and a Villain, so this is where you should start.

Traditionally, the Hero is a symbol of victory and positivity. The Hero can be a role model, a saviour or a champion. In contrast, the Villain symbolically plays the role of what opposes or obstructs the hero's quest. Often, therefore, the Villain takes the form of negativity, passivity, stasis and inertia – a failure to act, a fear of change and risk aversion.

The third role is that of the Mentor. The Mentor's role is to help the hero to achieve their Quest. Traditionally, they are the repository of knowledge, wisdom, calmness and reassurance. Often, they are the Wise Old Man – think of Obi-Wan Kenobi in the *Star Wars* films, Morpheus in *The Matrix*, Merlin in the Arthurian legends or Harry Potter's Dumbledore. Historically, they do tend to be more masculine.

Bear in mind this important point: it is tempting to automatically choose yourself, or your customer or company, as the Hero of your story, but at least resist the temptation to do so automatically. Why? Because the Hero and Villain do not necessarily have to be people. Often, I find this exercise works best when you choose an idea or a concept as the Hero and/or Villain.

To take one example, the 2008 Obama campaign featured a memorable poster designed by Shepard Fairey, emblazoned with one word: 'hope.' In the terms of this exercise, Obama was the Mentor, bringing the Hero ('hope,' 'progress' or 'change') to the people.

When I have done this exercise in workshops over the decades, some examples of the Heroes and Villains I have helped to nurture have included:

- Freedom (with the Villain embodied as convention, habit or orthodoxy)
- Bravery (with fear as the Villain)
- Purity (for the Greater London Authority, looking at air pollution as the Villain and one of the main health issues in the capital)
- Community/we (with 'I' as the anti-hero)
- Drive (with apathy or inertia as its antithesis)
- Home (vs the dark, unknown or alien 'outside')
- The light or a lighthouse (opposed by darkness or metaphorical ignorance)

RE-QUEST

Quests are the essence of heroism. They commonly feature a hero or protagonist who embarks upon a dangerous mission – often against all odds – to save a group of people or society. In many cases, the quest involves the Hero finding a symbolic object or person that they are duty bound to bring back home.

Classical examples abound, from the return of Odysseus to the labours of Hercules, Aeneas' departure from Troy and eventual foundation of Rome, and medieval stories such as *Sir Gawain and the Green Knight* and Sir Thomas Malory's *Le Morte d'Arthur*. More recently, there have been Frodo's journey to destroy the One Ring, Dorothy's quest to meet the Wizard in/of Oz, and Luke Skywalker's quest to destroy the Empire (and discover the secret of his parentage).

The original *Star Wars* films were actually very deliberately written as a Hero's journey, following the thinking of mythologist Joseph Campbell. George Lucas consulted Campbell often, and Campbell himself would later reference *Star Wars* as a good example of a contemporary Hero's journey.

Then we have Indiana Jones, Neo, Harry Potter, the parody *Monty Python and the Holy Grail* (1975) and *Tangled* (2010). In a marine context, we have *Finding Nemo* (2003), referencing Jules Verne's science-fiction adventure *Twenty Thousand Leagues Under the Seas* (1870) and the character of Captain Nemo, a scientific genius who roams the depths of the sea in his submarine in his quest for treasure, knowledge and revenge. Latterly, Dory has been sought too.

The philosopher Hannah Arendt emphasized the pre-eminence of meaning (and the search for meaning):

> The need of reason is not inspired by the quest
> for truth but by the quest for meaning. And meaning
> and truth are not the same.[44]

WEEK 5

Exercise 2

	Who – or what – is the Hero? It can be a person, group or idea	Who – or what – is the Villain? It can be a person, group or idea	What is their quest?	Who is the Mentor helping the Hero to achieve their quest? Is it you?
1				
2				
3				
4				

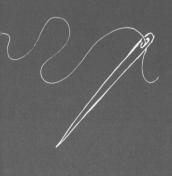

WEEK 6
SURPRISE!

	What you will learn	**What you will do**	**What that will lead to**
Week 6: Surprise!	Why surprise will help us evade attention spam	An exercise where you inject surprise and witness the results	Preparing for the last three ingredients

SURPRISE BRINGS
A SPECIAL KIND OF
FOCUSED ATTENTION.

We have established the importance of weaving our golden thread and appreciated that all stories need conflict. We now need to inject a certain amount of surprise into the proceedings.

I have always been a big fan of the power of hedgehogs...

... of surprise.

It was one of my key tips in *The Storytelling Book*, and my book on insight and inspiration, *The Inspiratorium*, devoted a significant chunk of space to the topic.[45] So, it should come as no surprise that I want to return to it here and help you to use the power of surprise.

Surprise stands at the heart of one of the biggest challenges we all face in cutting through attention spam (see Week 1): how do I get attention, and how do I keep it?

Andy Warhol said:

> My paintings never turn out the way I expect them, but I am never surprised.[46]

THE THRILL OF IT ALL

Surprise is thrilling.

We will cover this in more detail in Week 7, which looks at Robert Cialdini's work on mystery in academic papers. For now, consider the words of Tiffany Watt Smith, according to whom the uncertainty of surprise has a deep poignancy:

> Uncertainty, freedom, serendipity, whimsy, creativity: these are the delights of uncertainty. Not knowing an outcome can be immensely pleasurable – it's why we keep reading murder mysteries and why the first rush of a love affair is particularly intense.[47]

SOME SURPRISING SCIENCE

Information is rooted in surprise. We all function on the expectation that the world will work out in certain ways, but when it does, we're bored. The concept of expectation failure determines what we find it worthwhile to know. Our brain tends to become alert not when things *work* but when they *fail*. We learn something new when things don't turn out the way we expected.

One scientific point on surprise. The brain treats novelty, or surprising information, like a special kind of reward. The brain has evolved to reward us with pleasure for acquiring and understanding new information. Areas of the brain that become most active when we are trying to make sense of new information contain opioid receptors.

Scientist Robert Friedel said:

> The end of surprise would be the end of science. To this extent the scientist must constantly seek and hope for surprises.[48]

NOBODY EXPECTS

...the Spanish Inquisition. Surprise, as fans of Monty Python will recall, was the chief weapon of the Spanish Inquisition:

There is an arcane rhetorical term for sentences that start in one direction, take you where you expect to go, but then end up with a hedgehog. That term is – pause for emphasis – *paraprosdokian*, from the Greek for 'against expectation.' It denotes a sudden wrong-footing shift in meaning and/ or mood, and is at the heart of much comedy and satire.

Take this quote from the doyenne of the acerbic, Dorothy Parker:

> If all the girls who attended the Yale prom were laid end to end, I wouldn't be a bit surprised.[49]

Or this one from Douglas Adams's *The Hitchhiker's Guide to the Galaxy*:

> Trin Tragula – for that was his name – was a dreamer, a thinker, speculative philosopher, or as his wife would have it, an idiot.[50]

Before that, Groucho Marx was quite the exponent of the *paraprosdokian*:

> I've had a perfectly wonderful evening. But this wasn't it.[51]

Emo Philips is well known for his absurdist use of the tool:

> I like going to the park and watching the children run around because they don't know I'm using blanks.[52]

Or, even more darkly:

> I don't know why I got into trouble with my girlfriend's parents for not opening her car door. All I did was open mine and swim for the surface.[53]

Linked to the *paraprosdokian* is the 'garden-path sentence,' so called because it leads you down the 'garden path' of ambiguity.

Producer and comic writer John Lloyd (who produced, among other masterpieces, the radio adaptation of *The Hitchhiker's Guide to the Galaxy* and *Blackadder*) was interviewed by classicist Bettany Hughes for her BBC Radio 4 series *The Ideas That Make Us*. In the episode on comedy, she listens to the sound of rats laughing before exploring where comedy comes from and why it seems so universal and yet so little understood.

Laughter seems to be a social, mammal behaviour – more about conversation and being part of a tribal community than just about jokes.

Said Lloyd:

> Very often you are going along one path, it lures
> you down there and lures you along and suddenly
> everything explodes in a pun or surprise and your
> world is slightly changed. If we knew why things were
> funny, we'd know the answer to everything.

SURPRISE AS REFRAMING

The Prologue discussed the power of reframing: presenting logically equivalent information in a frame that makes us perceive and respond to that information in a different way.

As an example, consider arguably the most imaginative reframing of a classic movie, written for *TCM* by Rick Polito in 1998 and perhaps best described as strictly accurate but wholly misleading:

> Transported to a surreal landscape, a young girl kills
> the first person she meets and then teams up with
> three strangers to kill again.[54]

TOP TIPS

1. Respect the thrill of uncertainty – the core of whodunnits, murder mysteries and all the psychological thrillers we can't keep away from.

2. Pursue 'wow' rather than focusing on what is information rich.

3. If you never want to see or hear the word *paraprosdokian* again, keep calm: just create a garden path and show them a wilderness.

WEEK 6

Exercise

Pick up your material of choice and ask yourself
these questions:

	What are my audience expecting?	What can I say or do that would surprise them?
1		
2		

PART 3

ONTO THE
LAST LEG

So – deep breath – we have cleared the ground, understood the problem of attention spam, rid ourselves of turbulent jargon, gone through our SIMPLE checklist, and looked at the importance of weaving a thread, creating conflict and finding surprise.

This last stage of the tour is where we will look at and apply some aspects that will take your storytelling to the next level.

	What you will learn	What you will do	What that will lead to
Week 7: Grab Them Early	Why how we start (anything) is crucial to its memorability and impact	Exercises where you craft a killer opening line, and imagine a 'what if'	Linking structure will start to create a 'through-line'
Week 8: The Rule of Three	The power of three across all media	An exercise to enable you to practise with 'threes'	Approaching the finish line and preparing the killer headline
Week 9: Here Are the Headlines	Why headlines are concise, elegant and powerful	An exercise to highlight the difference between a title and a headline	Creating a knockout story based on all of the ingredients above

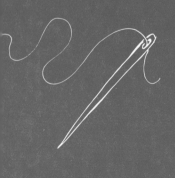

WEEK 7

GRAB THEM EARLY

	What you will learn	**What you will do**	**What that will lead to**
Week 7: Grab Them Early	Why how we start (anything) is crucial to its memorability and impact	Exercises where you craft a killer opening line, and imagine a 'what if'.	Linking structure with start to create a 'through-line'

HOW TO START?

Beginnings are not easy. The Nobel Prize-winning writer Gabriel García Márquez acknowledged that one of the hardest aspects of writing is the first paragraph.[55] He admitted that he would often spend many months on the first paragraph (so we shouldn't feel so bad about submitting that 500-word blog post).

But, on the positive side, once he 'got it,' the rest tumbled out easily. García Márquez admitted that writers solve most of the problems of their book in the first paragraph. The theme, the style and the tone are all settled. And, incidentally, this is exactly how we should represent our golden thread and produce our storyboard accordingly (see Week 4).

There is a tendency I have endured throughout much of my working life to start with something called (sometimes literally) the 'background.' Often this takes the form of what I call the 'Geography and History Section.' This happens when presentations are given that insist on committing at least two cardinal errors:

1. **Telling the audience what they already know, sometimes in depth:** Whether it's internal emails, a pitch presentation or a killer CV, there is an inherent tendency to start with a warm-up – a bit of shared banality such as "how great it would be to work with you" or "What did you think of United's performance at the weekend?"

2. **Giving too much basic 'geography and history':** The ad agency world, with which I am chronically over-familiar, is well known for its level of pitch frequency and intensity. There is too much emphasis on 'who we are, where we have offices and how we started.' Rather than this geography and history lesson, ad agencies should perhaps take some of their own medicine ('physician heal thyself') and understand their target audience. That means less emphasis on 'us' and more on 'you,' less focus on 'how wonderful we are' and more on 'how we can help you, O Client?'

Gordon Lish is an American writer, theorist and literary editor. Among his protégés were Don DeLillo, Ben Marcus and Diane Williams, and he is now perhaps best known to most readers as the editor who took a severe editorial pen to Raymond Carver's first two collections of stories.

Lish had a reputation for ruthless editing and was a proponent of what he called the "poetics of the sentence." One of his foundational precepts was the idea of the "attack sentence." He argued that it had to be as unexpected as it was dramatic.[56]

One of his former students tells of Lish calling for "an exorbitant opening sentence, a hook that hooks your reader to a line that could lead anywhere and everywhere."[57] Short story writer Amy Hempel remembers him pointing out the attack and "skipping past a page and a half of throat clearing to the real beginning of the story." This would demonstrate his belief in the need for "linguistic and thematic urgency."[58] For example, with Harold Brodkey's "His Son, In His Arms, In Light, Aloft" (1975), Lish put a red line through the original introductory paragraph, recommending instead that Brodkey start with the far more vivid:

> My father is chasing me.[59]

For Lish, when you create a sentence to follow the previous sentence, in a way, it becomes the new first attack sentence. "The sentence I'm putting down must contend with the prior sentence," he has been quoted as declaring.[60]

This sets the bar very high (even for literary practitioners, let alone those of us toiling in the paddy fields of business communication). However, that shouldn't deter us from attempting to write sentences, paragraphs, pages and charts that aspire to those lofty principles. And Lish's emphasis on excision and compression is something we could all learn from.

Hempel in turn became famous for her own attack sentences. Take, for example, the beginning of "The Harvest," the opening story in the first issue of *The Quarterly* (1987):

> The year I began to say vahz instead of vase, a man I barely knew nearly accidentally killed me.[61]

Lish also talked of "swerve" or "torque" to describe his theory that writing should twist and turn, surprise and disturb.[62]

SOME PEDAGOGIC MYSTERY TIME

Robert Cialdini has a special place among those of us in the academic–practitioner Venn diagram for being a guru in the field of social psychology and persuasion. Professor of psychology and marketing (we need more of these...) at Arizona State University, his 1984 book *Influence* was a game changer in introducing some of the key principles that lie beneath the surface in the areas of persuasion and influence. It regularly and rightly appears at the upper echelons of "smartest books" lists.

But I want to look at a paper he wrote in 2005, when he was trying to find the secret of a good lecture (lecturer, too, I'd vouch). Cialdini knew well enough from experience that the most common form of classroom lecture presentation usually involves the transmission of material that is relevant to the course.

Fair enough. A second approach is more interactive, asking students questions about this material. But was there something he was missing? Could a lecture be even more compelling?

As narrated in the wonderfully apposite and self-referential paper "What's the Best Secret Device for Engaging Student Interest? The Answer Is in the Title," he tried to find the answer.[63]

As a trainer, lecturer and parent, I can wholly identify with his challenge, and indeed his findings. Having sat in on too many lectures (and seen some experienced by my daughter – see the Prologue), I can testify that too many lecturers habitually feel that their job is merely to shift as much content as can be managed in 30, 40 or 60 minutes into the infinitely absorbent brains of their students. They seem to do this without any understanding of how it might be achieved without risking catatonia or a disgruntled walkout.

In looking at how academics typically try to appeal to and gain the attention of non-academics, Cialdini uncovered a number of truths.

Clarity and Structure

When examining all the different sections in paper, organizing them by type in what scientists are wont to call 'principal components analysis,' Cialdini discovered that the least successful were characterized (as you'd guess by now) by the absence of clarity and the prevalence of dull, jargonized prose.

The most successful pieces, though, tended to have a 'logical structure' (I'd call that the golden thread), vivid examples and (even?) humour.

Find the Mystery

But the real 'aha' moment for Cialdini was the discovery of one other deep-seated theme: all the best papers began with a *story*, and a *mystery* at that.

He tells the tale of an astronomer writing about the rings of Saturn, considered by scientists to be perhaps the most spectacular planetary feature in our solar system, and their composition. But even a star-struck (sorry) astronomer realized that the raw science – the neat undigested information – could be presented in a way that was far from alluring (lots of astro-technical terms, numbers, etc.) Instead, the author chose to introduce the topic with a series of questions. As the mystery deepened, he revealed that three different groups of specialists (why always three?) had different explanations – gas, dust particles or ice crystals.

After 20 pages of keeping his audience in suspense (running rings around them, you could say), he reveals 'whodunit': it is dust, but with a bit of ice in there too.

In itself, that could have been rather flat. However, the author had created a story, built around a mystery that begs to be answered or 'closed.' It almost doesn't matter *how* niche, *how* technical, *how* remote the topic or information is from its intended audience – creating a mystery, posing a question or leaving something unanswered is a sure-fire way to gain interest and attention. And, lest it need to be stated, this is all without any gratuitous gimmickry. It works with the natural processes of the brain.

Recall – the astronomer made the mystery last for 20 pages. If you're dubious about that, think about how many episodes of your favourite binge-watch you can sustain before you reach the final resolution or revelation. My only exception is the TV series *Lost* (2004–2010).

Cialdini employed the technique himself. He gives one example of a lesson where he set up his own mystery. He got his timings in a tangle and found the bell had gone before he had revealed the answer. Instead of the students packing up their pencils and leaving, he was (in his words) "pelted with protests." Cialdini talks about how this approach creates a 'huh?' before the final 'aha!' Mysteries, as he states, demand explanations.

Finally, he gives us his – surprisingly story-friendly – plan for executing the mystery-story sequence:

- Pose the mystery
- Deepen the mystery
- Offer some alternative explanations
- Provide clues
- Resolve the mystery
- Draw out the implications from the story

A story is, at its heart, an answer to two questions: What happens next? And how will it turn out? Therefore, as Cialdini concludes, the mystery, the puzzle or the enigma is something to be actively sought out, rather than avoided. This is something that Cialdini feels, on its face, may seem in defiance of logic or common sense.

Every story at its heart is a detective story, whether it's a straightforward thriller or a whodunnit. From what was perhaps Western literature's first detective story – Oedipus seeking the answer to who killed his father – to the modern craze for 'true crime' TV series and podcasts, we can appreciate the power inherent in the puzzle, the mystery and the enigma.

THE MYSTERY BOX

The idea of a mysterious box has appeared many times in literature and popular culture:

- In *The Storytelling Book*, I referred to J J Abrams's story of his 'mystery box,' a box given to him by his grandfather marked with a question mark on the outside. Abrams made it a personal mission to never open it and let the mystery master knowledge.[64]
- Freud wrote a paper about mysterious boxes and caskets (they appear in Shakespeare, for example).[65]
- One classical example comes from book ten of Homer's *Odyssey*. Odysseus receives the bag of Aeolus, which contains all the storm winds and can ensure his safe voyage home. But Odysseus' sailors are too curious, greedy and stupid. They believe that the bag contains treasure that Odysseus is hiding from them. When they are in sight of their homeland, Ithaca, and Odysseus is forced to take a brief nap, they open the bag up. The adverse winds pour out, which forces them wildly off course. A warning against the perils of temptation, perhaps.

For many, especially in the domain of psycho-analysis, the mystery box is the black box of the unconscious. Strangely for us layfolk, the black box recorder on planes is actually orange (as anyone will know if they watched the last season of *Homeland*, 2011–2020), but the symbolism trumps the science.

Honestly Assess Your Material

One other insight resonated for me. Why was it that in Cialdini's analysis, natural scientists seemed more prone to using this technique than social or behavioural scientists? Surely the latter should be better versed in human behaviour and communication theory? His best guess (and I think it's on the button) was that behavioural scientists suffer from the smug confidence that their content is so intrinsically interesting that it needs no added 'embellishment.' And maybe natural scientists are more honest about the limitations of their material and are subject to no such self-delusion.

Hands up: which category are you in? How many of us (and how often) do we feel that the sheer weight and majesty of what we have to say is – or should be – tasty enough bait to reel in our audience?

TOP TIPS

1. Don't just throat-clear, ramble and stumble into what you are saying, writing or promising. Create that attack sentence – cast the hook that baits your listeners.

2. Follow the wisdom of Gordon Lish and actively seek a swerve or torque.

3. Keep the history and geography lesson to a minimum.

4. Mystery and question, puzzle and enigma are not to be feared or shunned but to be encouraged. They are the best way to emotionally engage people with your material.

WEEK 7

Exercise 1

1. Grab your upcoming presentation or talk, or that rather inert CV, or even your Tinder profile.

2. Craft a killer opening line that will knock your audience dead (ideally not literally) and mark you indelibly in their minds.

3. Make sure it packs an emotional punch and is free of jargon.

4. Can you make it short enough to remember and rehearse?

WHAT IF?

One of the great advantages of being conscious animals is that we can imagine a future.

We alone have the ability to conjure up hypotheses, to build models of the future for ourselves, our close ones or the world. And we can recalibrate our thoughts and actions based on that speculation. To let our hypotheses die in our stead, as Karl Popper put it, is one of our species' defining characteristics.[66]

This is a form of cognitive play – the sort of playfulness that is essential to creativity.

Stories play a role (as it were) in this – one that perhaps has evolutionary origins and adaptive advantages. Namely, stories can act as rehearsals for life and prepare us to explore possibility as much as reality, enhancing our capacity to predict, interpret and respond to events. This sort of 'playful pretence' is also claimed by games-makers, who argue that many of the best video games are microcosms – alternative realities that allow us to indulge our impulse to explore.

Hypothesis-making is the heart of the scientific enterprise as much as it is of creative domains. Many theorists argue that the evolutionary role of all storytelling and drama is about training us to explore possibility as well as actuality. This improves our capacity to interpret and respond to events, and it enhances our chances of fruitful reproduction.

Science fiction in particular operates in a number of ways that underpin the popularity of the genre both as entertainment and as philosophical investigation. It can work as:

- **Prognostication:** imagining worlds that are ostensibly alien or distant, but are actually our world but explored from another perspective. H G Wells was a prime exponent of this approach.
- **Projection:** this uses an idea that science-fiction writer and pioneer of cyberpunk William Gibson formulated in various interviews: "The future is already here – it's just not evenly distributed."[67] As well as providing fertile ground for philosophical meandering, the idea can be a great source of speculation and imagination. For example, think about the degree to which debates around robots, AI and the human–computer interface have been aired in the pages of sci-fi writers from Isaac Asimov to Arthur C Clarke to Gibson and Alex Garland. So much of sci-fi fits under the umbrella of parable, too. Take, for example, George Orwell's *Animal Farm* (1945). Whether Margaret Atwood's *The Handmaid's Tale* (1985) fits into this sci-fi genre is a vexed topic that I intend to steer clear of completely.

So, why can we not use this simple trick more? In the research and insight world in which I often dwell, hypothesis is still underused.

In training people about the principles and practice of marketing, I use the term 'hypothesis' a lot. This is because at the heart of marketing theory and practice is the following model: 'What if we selected these people, and addressed them in this way, and hoped to change their behaviour to this end?'

In the same way that science fiction can operate by creating alternative universes, so should we use this approach to benefit our documents, presentations or CVs. Looked at from this perspective, the process of deriving a marketing and targeting strategy is best done through the lens of storytelling.

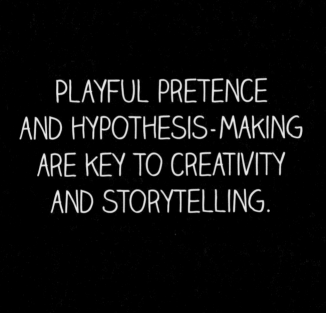

PLAYFUL PRETENCE
AND HYPOTHESIS-MAKING
ARE KEY TO CREATIVITY
AND STORYTELLING.

WEEK 7

Exercise 2

Pick the version (or versions) of this exercise that applies to your own context.

YOU WORK IN MARKETING, COMMUNICATIONS OR RESEARCH

Formulate your presentation and give it bite by asking and answering these questions:

1. What if we try a new targeting strategy? What if we examine the positioning of the brand – the classic 'what market are we in/could we be in/should we be in'?

2. What if we try to reframe the brand away from its current perception or market location?

3. What if we go all out for identifying an insight that transforms the brand?

4. What might 'alternative realities' for the brand or comms look like?

YOU ARE WORKING ON A SPEECH OR PRESENTATION

Write down what you would do and say differently if you asked:

1. What if my speech didn't take up all the allotted time (but only, say, half the time)?

2. What if I chose not to use PowerPoint?

3. What if I gave myself other arbitrary constraints, such as one word per chart? No words at all? Only using book titles or names of films?

4. What if I left all the data and information in a separate deck – what would I want to say and show?

YOU WANT TO REFRESH YOUR CV OR JOB APPLICATION

Ask yourself:

1. What if I my audience, interviewer or date had only five seconds, or I met them in the lift?

2. What if I had to avoid using words?

3. What if the only thing I had to do was turn myself into the most distinctive candidate?

4. What if I stopped thinking about what I wanted to say and focused on the other person?

5. What if I could do something in this job that I hadn't thought of or expected?

YOU WANT TO TAKE ANOTHER LOOK AT YOUR TINDER PROFILE

1. What if I thought of myself as a brand? What brand of car, airline, social media network or chocolate bar would I be?

2. What if I acknowledged (or even emphasized) my weaknesses, to make myself look less perfect and more human and fallible?

3. What if I created my profile just using pictures, emojis, my favourite films, books, sports or celebrities?

WEEK 8

THE RULE
OF THREE

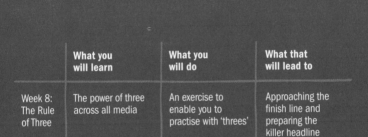

	What you will learn	What you will do	What that will lead to
Week 8: The Rule of Three	The power of three across all media	An exercise to enable you to practise with 'threes'	Approaching the finish line and preparing the killer headline

WHY IS THE NUMBER THREE SO SPECIAL?

Three, according to the song, is a magic number. Written in 1973 by Bob Dorough on the US educational children's series *Schoolhouse Rock!*, it has been sampled and revived regularly since then – most notably by De La Soul in 1990. It was even used for the UK's National Lottery advertising campaign in late 2019.

It does seem that there is something mysterious and potent about the number three.

To find out why, let's dig a little deeper by examining the concept known as 'chunking.' When I am training or lecturing on behavioural economics (and sometimes more broadly on theories of how communication works), I always reserve some time for chunking. At its simplest, chunking is the principle that the brain resents and rejects vast tracts of undifferentiated material (this material is designated as what I call 'attention spam' – see Week 1). The way to avoid this is by chunking: breaking large things down into smaller segments or chunks.

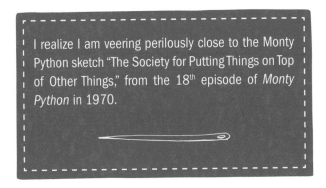

I realize I am veering perilously close to the Monty Python sketch "The Society for Putting Things on Top of Other Things," from the 18th episode of *Monty Python* in 1970.

Chunking is something that is almost too trivially obvious to ignore, yet ignored it most frequently is. When you look at a homepage, utility bill, mobile phone plan, CV, document or presentation, how apparent is it that the principle of chunking is being blatantly disregarded?

Chunking is – or should be – used in all sorts of circumstances.

Having worked with pharmaceutical companies, I have seen that compliance is one of the toughest challenges for healthcare professionals. Many patients have a complicated regime of medicines to organize throughout the day, and taking the right ones at the right times (known as compliance) is clearly deeply important. This is why, in the cause of encouraging this compliance, all sorts of techniques are devised: from allocating different times of the day to devising different compartments for separating pills to colour-coding medicines. Again, this is about chunking something long and complicated (many medicines with many different effects, to be consumed at different times) so that the process of selection is made easier.

Here is a list – chunked into three – of some conclusions and implications of chunking:

- **Parts are easier to digest than wholes:** Break bigger things down into smaller sections, use more paragraphs, add more white space (as any ad person will attest). And, when speaking, use... more... pauses... to accentuate what is important.
- **The way a task is presented affects our willingness to take it on and complete it:** Elsewhere I talk (drone on about) the obsession we have with content (what we say) at the expense of form (how we say it). As we saw in the Prologue, framing indicates the importance of the 'how' – the need to reflect as much on the delivery as on the content. So, in the compliance example above, how the task of taking the medication is presented has a drastic effect on the likelihood of patients following it religiously (even if it is a matter of life and death).
- **Recall:** Chunking aids recall of information, amongst other outcomes.

One final example, again from the healthcare world. In 2009, the UK health sector created a campaign to help people recognize the signs of someone having a stroke. The tagline is "When a stroke strikes, act FAST." This is a simple, memorable acronym for "Face. Arms. Speech. Time." The acronym acts as the first chunk. Then, after that in a second chunk, more information nestles:

- **Facial weakness:** Can they smile? Has their mouth or eye drooped?
- **Arm weakness:** Can they raise both arms?
- **Speech problems:** Can they speak clearly, and can they understand what you're saying?
- **Time:** It's time to call 999 immediately if you see any of these symptoms.

WHY THREE?

The science behind the number three has quite a story in itself.

The go-to paper on memory retention was written by George Miller back in 1956.[68] Note to film fans: this is not the same (Australian) George Miller who wrote and directed the *Mad Max* movies (1979–2015) and was also involved with *Babe* (1995) and co-wrote and directed *Happy Feet* (2006).

The paper – "The Magical Number Seven, Plus or Minus Two" – discussed the idea that memory span is limited to two or three bits or seven items. It is one of the most cited in psychology, partly perhaps because it was written with no little humour and whimsy (Miller describes himself as "being persecuted by an integer").

More recently in what I now considered to be a seminal paper – "The Magical Mystery Four: How Is Working Capacity Limited, and Why?" (2010) – Nelson Cowan, a psychologist at the University of Missouri, argued that "there truly is a central working memory faculty limited to 3 to 5 chunks for adults, which can predict mistakes in thinking and reasoning."[69]

Experts define working memory as the 'temporarily active' thoughts people can keep in their head at any given moment. This type of memory tends to come in handy when we are reading (to retain ideas presented earlier in a text), for solving problems and even in short-term planning.

THREE-THINKING

In *The Storytelling Book*, I gave a few examples of famous threes and their ubiquity.[70] They are especially populous in fairy tales (Billy Goats Gruff, bears, blind mice and little pigs) and also appear in literature (musketeers), religion (wise men, and the Father, the Son and the Holy Spirit) and mantras. They are also seen in law ("the truth, the whole truth and nothing but the truth"), political slogans ("lies, damn lies and statistics," "Education Education Education") and TV shows (*Location, Location, Location*). Brands too have jumped onto the brand-wagon (from the Mars bar's memorable "work, rest and play" to Chevrolet's "eye it, try it and buy it" in the 1930s and 1940s). I have a particular fondness for the track by Ian Dury, "Sex & Drugs & Rock & Roll."

Then, of course, we have the phenomenon known as the TLA (three-letter acronym). It's not unfair to say that there is an epidemic of them, but again the power of three seems to add power wherever it is applied.

At this point, British readers may want to skip ahead, as I want to look at the power of three as used in recent political events. This will necessitate the use of the 'B' word.

Because, leaving political affiliation aside (clue: I live in North London, shop at Waitrose, and speak French and some Italian), we can dispassionately analyse the way that communications for Br*xit were firmly rooted in an understanding of the rule of three.

In order to cut through the confusion and apathy surrounding the issue of Br*xit ahead of the referendum, the Leave camp designed a slogan:

Take Back Control.

I well remember at the time thinking both "how very smart" (professionally) and "oh dear" (personally). Even without hindsight, it seemed a well-thought-out attempt to define the issue for a particular constituency (this is Marketing 101). Let's analyse it in three (naturally) ways.

Firstly, the noun 'control': who doesn't want to feel they are in control? One of the essential characteristics of the human condition is known (technically) as 'agency': the sense that we have power and influence in the world. Another even more erudite term is 'effectance': our ability to have an impact or effect on our surroundings.

Secondly, the idea of 'taking back' control was a very subtle attempt to identify some of the issues swirling around the Br*xit debate, especially on the Leave side. It implicitly addressed what was at the heart of the Leave argument: the feeling that 'we' (the people) had lost control, and that it had been taken away. For some it had been taken away by a tide of immigrants entering the country; in another sense, control and autonomy had been weakened or even eliminated by the bureaucrats at the heart of the European Union. "Back" is key – so much more emphatic than 'taking control.' Again, let me emphasize, I am trying to remain relatively impartial and only examine the slogan through the lens of communication theory.

Thirdly, the slogan uses the form of the verb called the imperative – the 'do!' form. In the comms world, this has traditionally been known as the 'call to action.' This is where, having been embraced, coddled and seduced by the emotional wrapping of an ad, the customer is confronted with a thinly veiled commandment to go and buy. So, it feels very direct: 'take it back now,' the slogan exhorts us.

More recently – hang in there, we're coming to the end of the Br*xit section – after the referendum and in the ensuing chaos, the Conservative Party campaigned in the 2019 general election under the line "Get Brexit Done." *Time* magazine went as far as to say that "it was clear those three words had helped win Boris Johnson's party an overwhelming majority."[71]

As with all these things, untangling the various threads of cause and effect is a labyrinthine task. However, most commentators agree that the slogan – another three-word imperative – was immensely effective. Like the Leave slogan, it was simple and effective, and it crystallized a huge amount of emotional baggage: this time not just corralling the Leavers to vote for the party that would unequivocally guarantee delivering Br*xit but also – almost subliminally – appealing to Remainers who had reached the end of their patience and were just happy to get (Br*x)it out of the way ("done") so they could get back to their lives.

Interestingly, a number of people who read or reread *The Storytelling Book* have pointed out a word I used. I was arguing that all blends of words – like Brangelina or Jedward – tend to be grotesque failures. The word I used at the time to talk about the political situation was... Grexit. I wrote the manuscript at the end of 2014 and in early 2015, and at that time it was Greece's financial and economic uncertainty that was in the news. Br*xit –though the term had already been coined – was still a dim and distant shadow on the political horizon. How times change...

The UK government's communications when responding to COVID-19 in 2020 were equally built out of three components: "Stay Home, Protect the NHS, Save Lives."

And, for American readers and watchers of US politics, "Make America Great Again," though not exactly a three-word mantra, shares much of the characteristics of its UK equivalents. A simple, unsophisticated verb ("Make"), like "Take" and "Get," is a direct patriotic call and gives a sense of reviving past glories. Just like taking back control was about restoring autonomy, so making America great again was about re-establishing a link to a past that was perhaps idealized, but potent nonetheless.

THE MAGIC NUMBER
THREE IS THE BEGINNING,
MIDDLE AND END OF
STORYTELLING.

TOP TIPS

1. Try never to allow yourself to make more than three points on a slide, in a chart or in a paragraph. The cognitive limits we have been discussing give an unambiguous verdict: the brain can just about take in and recall three items. Bear this in mind across all your communications, from your CV to your Tinder profile. Especially guilty are those who insist that they have "11 things I have to absolutely land" in a presentation. (And don't get me started on the jargonistic 'land.')

2. Infographics are popular, but turning numbers into pictures is not a guarantee of memorability and impact. Too often I see people (typically researchers) assume that by combining lots of output into one slide but prettifying it, they will garner my attention. As a Manchester United fan, I receive regular updates from the team on social media, often in the form of infographics. They give the appearance of being easy to digest because they are full of pretty images and colours. However, there is still too much information to take in.

3. The most important (I refrained from using 'life-changing' there) aspect of three is this: it aids memory. I propose the following plan to help you remember a presentation, document or speech, or to use in finding a job or a mate.

a. Divide your material into three. This will help as you develop your golden thread and build your story-board (see Week 4).
b. Next, give each of the three sections a title or better still a headline (see Week 9). This can be a word, a name, an image, an object or a metaphor. But it should be both a pertinent summary of that section and memorably brief.
c. Then all you have to do is recall those three words, images or names and you will find that your brain can reconstruct a large proportion of your entire 20-minute speech, 30-minute presentation or three-page CV.

This can be a really useful trick to cover yourself against emergencies. Though tech has made significant improvements in recent years, there are still times where you will find yourself at the mercy of the Mighty USB God of Tech and Chaos. And there will be times when, as a student or presenter, or in a meeting, the gods see you as Sisyphus and curse you to forever try rebooting your laptop. This is when you will thank me and the rule of three: if the screen won't light up or you've lost your papers, those three words or images will be a life-saver.

WHAT, SO WHAT, NOW WHAT?

I want to end this topic by focusing on one particular three-based approach – one with a great deal of power. This is an approach to creating a golden thread based on the power of three in a model devised in a rather unexpected place: the book *Critical Reflection in Nursing and the Helping Professions: A User's Guide* by Gary Rolfe and colleagues.[72]

Rolfe is emeritus professor of nursing at Swansea University and the book is described as a text intended to provide nurses and other health care professionals with a guide to all aspects of reflective practice. The brilliance of the model has ensured that it has been adopted far and wide, especially in business and management circles, among which most people probably have no idea of its emphatically non-commercial origins.

The book has quite an academic slant (the word 'paradigm' occurs a lot, which is never a good sign). However, the heart of the model is wonderfully relevant to any form of presentation or argument. It is based on acknowledging and then answering three simple questions:

- What?
- So what?
- Now what?

I commend this model to you for consideration when you have something to analyse, develop or present.

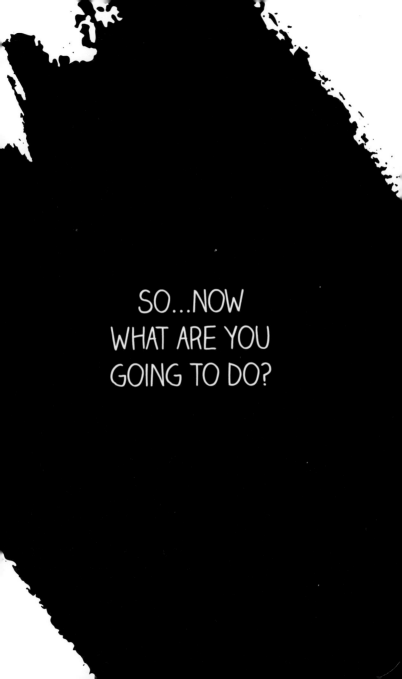

WEEK 8

Exercise

Now, take your document of choice and ask these questions of it:

WHAT?

1. Describe the particular situation, then focus on achievements, consequences, responses, feelings and any problems

2. Consider:

a. What is the real problem or issue you are facing?

b. What happened?

c. What did you notice (that was surprising)?

d. How did everyone react?

e. How did this compare to what you or they expected?

f. What positive or negative aspects did you observe?

SO WHAT?

Ask why it was so significant – what was the impact? Then consider:

1. Why is it important?

2. What critical questions does this information cause you to ask?

3. What emotions does it evoke for you? How does it make you feel?

4. What conclusions can be drawn?

NOW WHAT?

Here you identify what you need to do in the future in order to improve future outcomes and develop your learning:

1. What have you really learned?

2. How will you do things differently?

3. What – if anything – was the insight that will change how you do business, see yourself, see the world or change your client's point of view?

Finally, I sometimes use my own streamlined version of Rolfe, which I call the 'three Is' – issues, impact and implications:

- Outline a key **issue** (about the project you are working on, the speech you have to give or how you want to distinguish yourself on a dating app). Have a point of view and find a direction.
- What is the **impact** of this on the business, the future, the 'consumer' or your ideal role or date?
- Finally, what are the **implications**? What does this mean, what changes will you make or propose, and how will people see you (or your client, their business, their brand) differently?

TOP TIPS

1. Parts beat wholes: keep chunking and smashing wholes into smaller pieces – this can include acronyms

2. Remember the limits of short-term memory and how three can help in this regard

3. If I may use the term, keep three-basing

WEEK 9

HERE ARE THE HEADLINES

	What you will learn	What you will do	What that will lead to
Week 9: Here Are the Headlines	Why headlines are concise, elegant and powerful	An exercise to highlight the difference between a title and a headline	Creating a knockout story based on all of the ingredients above

We have now prepared a framework for storytelling. Among other things, we have established our foundational criteria, delved into the fabric of weaving a thread and using a storyboard, and examined the importance of three. Now it is time for the last stage: once we have started to develop our thread, found our conflict, adopted the element of surprise and looked at our storyboard, we must develop a headline.

Having found through Ancestry.co.uk that I am genetically 27% adman (technically, advertising is 67% aspiration, 23% inspiration and 10% desperation), I cannot help but revert to type(face) and promote the power of a good headline. As David Ogilvy says:

> On average, five times as many people read the headline as read the body copy. When you have written your headline, you have spent eighty cents out of your dollar.[73]

But I'd prefer not to use the word 'title.' Instead, let's call them 'headlines.' Then we can see why titles are not just any old words stitched together to put at the start of our presentation, speech, CV or Tinder profile.

But let me be clear about the semantic boundary here. A title is – in the sense I am referring to – a description, tending towards the factual, arid and reductive. In contrast, a headline is simple, provocative and memorable.

So, as all journalists and advertising copywriters will tell you, a good headline is worth its weight in communication gold.

(This partly explains why copywriters and newspaper sub-editors are traditionally well-paid.)

Headlines are the zenith of writing at its simplest and most essentialist. Creativity is to a large extent consonant with simplicity, which we know the brain prefers to complexity. Less is more: we prefer less information, so the longer the explanation, the less we trust it. Edward de Bono called simplicity "a unification around a purpose."[74]

That is why scientists link beauty and elegance with a formal scientific simplicity. It is also why the movie about the life of the games theorist (and Russell Crowe lookey-likey) John Nash was called *A Beautiful Mind* (2001) rather than, say, *A Complex Mind* or (if he had worked in market research) *An Insightful Mind*.

Yet many of us (especially in the business sphere) seem to have a love–hate relationship with headlines. Perhaps this is because they appeal to the emotions and thus bring with them a fear of being seduced or brainwashed. Or maybe it's because they have been tainted by associations with advertising, spin and the recent onslaught of 'fake news.' Or it might just be that we fear brevity leads to omission, simplification and distortion.

But surely, as with any form of communication, channel or even technology, headlines are not in themselves 'bad.' The key is to understand how they are designed and intended to be consumed.

WHAT ARE THE KEY CRITERIA
FOR A GOOD HEADLINE?

Experts will give different verdicts on what makes a good headline. However, from years of exploring, researching and responding to headlines, my own guidelines are as follows (incidentally, these also apply to chart and slide titles):

Let Simplicity Be Your Watchword

You'd expect nothing less from me, but I believe headlines are a form of compression of expression. The headline is the essential summary, synthesis and core of *what* you are attempting to communicate (and, no less importantly, *how*). If you need to beef this point up with scientific heft, you can assert that you are availing yourself of an extremely powerful discipline to enhance cognitive ease.

Keep It Brief

The optimum number of words is between six and ten. However, this 'norm' was parodied by a famous *Economist* poster campaign developed in the 1980s by Abbott Mead Vickers (this particular execution was produced in 2000):

> A poster should contain no more than eight words, which is the maximum the average reader can take in at a single glance. This, however, is for Economist readers.[75]

David Ogilvy claimed that the best headline he wrote was 18 words long: "At Sixty Miles an Hour the Loudest Noise in the New Rolls-Royce Comes from the Electric Clock."[76]

The idea of brevity has also been neatly skewered by Daniel Oppenheimer, currently professor of psychology at Carnegie Mellon University. In 2006, he wrote a paper in the journal *Applied Cognitive Psychology* in which he explored the tendency (especially prevalent amongst students) to try to 'beef up' their texts by needlessly employing long, ostentatiously pretentious (yes, I know) words. His study suggested a counterintuitive effect: people who try to use complexity to display their intelligence create the opposite impression. In his study, those who wrote clearly and simply were judged as smart, whereas those who used needlessly long words came across as less intelligent and less confident. The title of his paper? "Consequences of Erudite Vernacular Utilized Irrespective of Necessity: Problems with Using Long Words Needlessly."[77]

Be Provocative

Headlines are designed to be provocative. This is a key concept that runs throughout this book like, well, a golden thread (see Week 4). If what we are saying, writing or declaiming is not built on the drive to provoke something (a reaction, a response, a rethinking), then why are we doing it at all?

The word has received some negative attention of late. However, rather than fearing being provocative, we should use it as our watchword.

That means employing emotional appeals, using our friend surprise (see Week 6) and resisting the temptation to resort to dry, dusty, ossified language. No one is going to salivate at the prospect of a presentation titled "Automotive Sales by Region, 2007–2019." This is not merely because it reeks of generic meaninglessness and breeds apathy, but also because it gives no *clue*. If your headline fails to either cause an emotional response or give the audience a hint of what to expect, you have doubly failed.

Be Creative

There is no absolute mandate as to what is 'correct' – no black and white. As ever, try to put yourself in the mind of your reader, audience, employer-to-be or potential life partner.

There may be literary allusions or other cultural codes or references that work precisely because they show you understand your audience. But there may be cultural, geographical or other reasons why a reference might be lost or – worse still – counterproductive.

Similarly, if you think your audience will be sensitive to puns or word play, go ahead. Or, if they are punaphobic, maybe look elsewhere.

SOME MEMORABLE HEADLINES

Newspapers

As someone steeped in ad headlines, it's hard for me to pluck a few out for special mention. But here are a few favourites:

- The *Los Angeles Times* came up with a cracker in May 2013: "Big Rig Carrying Fruit Crashes on 210 Freeway, Creates Jam."[78]
- Another well-preserved headline, from the *Daily Telegraph* in February 2017, is "Marmalade Is the Preserve of the Elderly, Data Shows."[79]
- The most famous headline in US press history is often accorded to "Headless Body in Topless Bar" from the *New York Post* in April 1983 and written by Vincent A Musetto.[80] The anecdote (as recounted by Charlie Carillo, who was in the newsroom at the time) is worth retelling in its full lurid glory:

"Hang on, Vinnie, we're not a hundred per cent sure it's a topless bar!"

Vinnie jumped on top of his desk and waved his arms.

"It's gotta be a topless bar!" he cried. "This is the greatest f------ headline of my career!"

Vinnie got his wish. The topless bar angle checked out, and within minutes the presses were rolling.[81]

- *The Onion* has produced a collection of brilliant head-lines. I have an especial fondness for "Drugs Win Drugs War" from January 1998.[82]

Books

Book titles have gradually been adopting some of these principles.

One of my most cherished book titles was that of a work on artificial intelligence. In 1979, writer and journalist Pamela McCorduck wrote *Machines Who Think*. That 'who' gives you a clue as to the core issue at the heart of the book: what is the boundary between a thing, an insensate object or machine (a 'what') and a sentient, complex human being (a 'who')?

And no, headlines don't always have to be verbally clever. A reprint of George Orwell's *Nineteen Eighty-Four* used a striking visual approach. The designer, David Pearson, used obliteration and debossing to effectively black out the title and the author's name: a metaphor for the censorship at the heart of Orwell's work.[83]

Since 1978, there has even been an award for the oddest (I like to think 'most distinctive') book title of the year. The Bookseller/Diagram Prize does keep its tongue fairly ensconced in its cheek, but it is a reminder of the power of memorability. A few of the best are *How to Avoid Huge Ships* (John W Trimmer, 1982), *Greek Rural Postmen and Their Cancellation Numbers* (Derek Willan, 1994),

Living with Crazy Buttocks (Kaz Cooke, 2001), *Managing a Dental Practice: The Genghis Khan Way* (Michael R Young, 2010) and *Cooking with Poo* (the nickname of the Bangkok-based chef Saiyuud Diwong, 2011).

2013 was a vintage year: *Goblinproofing One's Chicken Coop* (Reginald Bakeley, 2012) was victorious, pushing the prize further into the public's purview. It edged out the likes of *How Tea Cosies Changed the World* (Loani Prior, 2012), *God's Doodle: The Life and Times of the Penis* (Tom Hickman, 2012) and – this still raises a giggle – *Lofts of North America: Pigeon Lofts* (Jerry Gagne, 2010). This is still available at https://foyspetsupplies.com/lofts-of-north-america/

But it is hard to see beyond the inaugural winner: 1978's *Proceedings of the Second International Workshop on Nude Mice* (Tatsuji Nomura and colleagues, 1977).

Before we laugh this away, it is worth considering the possibility that we do sometimes judge a book by its cover. Some books with *outré* titles may owe at least some of their success to their unusual monikers.

I offer as evidence Marina Lewycka's *A Short History of Tractors in Ukrainian* (2005), which has sold over a million copies worldwide. Another is *The Guernsey Literary and Potato Peel Pie Society* by Mary Ann Shaffer and Annie Barrows (2008), which hit number one on the *New York Times* bestseller list and was made into a movie in 2018.

Placards and Campaigns

Finally, placards at protests and demonstrations often display genuine ingenuity, and political ads can do too. Here are some examples:

- One from a Br*xit-related demonstration in 2019, written in typically dry and understated British style: "I'm not one to make a fuss usually, but the past couple of years have been quite farcical really."
- Compare and contrast this with an American cardboard sign carried by Jim Crocamo of New York City: "Not usually a sign guy, but Jeez." A protest against President-Elect Trump in November 2016, it became (of course) a short-lived meme.
- In 2014 a Filipino politician, Jun-jun Sotto, created perhaps the most honest political ad in campaigning history: "I'll do my best but I can't promise anything." The naked honesty is what is so shocking here.

ADDING ZEST

So, now you need to compose your own legendary (okay, let's settle for memorable) headline. Here is some help before you do.

Here are some 'before and after' examples of presentation headlines, duly anonymized to protect the guilty. On the left is the original (yawn) and on the right is how I have tried to add a little zest.

"Core Brand Relaunch Presentation"	"The 3 Cs: Confusion, Clarity and Consistency"
"March 2017 Quarterly Colleague Audit"	"Keeping Colleagues Happy to Keep Customers Happy"
"Internal Comms Update"	"Letting Them Know Not Letting Them Down"
"Exploring Competitive Strategic Options for Project H"	"Landing the Killer Blow?"
"End-of-Year Quarterly Analysis"	"Who Won Christmas?!"

The first uses the rule of three and some good old alliteration.

The second makes clear the essence of the report – that in order to keep consumers satisfied, staff needed to feel valued too.

The third – another internal communications study – alludes to the belief that the staff in question felt left out of company decisions.

The fourth example began life as a typically generically, mundane headline for a marketing exercise. The company I was consulting for had attempted to launch a promotion to price one of its rivals out of the market. We decided to use a boxing metaphor to encapsulate the issue: did the company knock out its rival, or did it administer the killer blow to itself?

And finally, why use the tired, tiresome and tedious "End-of-Year Quarterly Analysis" when you can lure your audience by promising the answer to the only question anyone cares about: "Who Won Christmas?!"

Now, over to you...

THINK OF YOUR HEADLINE
AS THE TITLE OF – OR
TRAILER FOR – A MOVIE.
WOULD IT MAKE YOU
WANT TO GO SEE IT?

WEEK 9

Exercise

Try your hand at writing a headline for your document of choice. But don't just write one. Try out a few and test them on colleagues, friends and family.

	Headline	is it six to ten words long?	Does it sum up and crystallize your golden thread?	Is it memorable and enduring?
Headline 1				
Headline 2				
Headline 3				

AND NOW, THE END

I hope you've found the path to becoming a storyteller both informative and rewarding.

If you'll permit me, I will end by expanding on the idea of the path. Alongside the golden thread, I hope this is one of the abiding images you will take from this workbook (see Week 4).

To do this, I'd like to evoke an image of an elephant and a rider. This metaphor was first elucidated by a social psychologist and professor of ethical leadership at New York University's Stern School of Business, Jonathan Haidt, in his *The Happiness Hypothesis* (2006).

Haidt used the analogy of an elephant and a rider to describe the two thinking processes, also popularized by Daniel Kahneman in his much lauded *Thinking, Fast and Slow* (2011). Kahneman borrowed the terms System 1 and System 2 to describe and differentiate between our two independent systems of thinking. System 2 is the cold, slow and rational process, and System 1 (which is far more important than we like to think) is the home of our unconscious emotional side. In Haidt's book, the elephant is System 1 (the unconscious, emotive instinctual force) while System 2 is the rider perched on top and clinging on in the illusory belief that they are actually the one in control. And often the rider and elephant are actively hostile to each other.

In the hands of academics Chip and Dan Heath, this metaphor becomes even deeper and more imaginative. In their book *Switch: How to Change Things When Change Is Hard* (2010), they talk about directing messages to the rational rider and the emotional elephant. However, they add a third (of course) element: the notion of the path. The path, in their retelling, is the route that can help the two systems work in tandem. So, change is most likely to occur when all three elements work together: when the rider can direct the elephant down a well-prepared path.

In language that echoes the messages from the UK government during the COVID-19 pandemic (see Week 8), we might think of this approach as "Direct the Rider, Motivate the Elephant, Shape the Path."

I hope I have addressed each of these components in this workbook. I hope your rider feels they have learned many tips, tricks and techniques that you can put into practice immediately and easily. I trust that your instinctive, unconscious elephant feels the sense of reward, satisfaction and achievement that comes with the application of new insights. And my aim has also been to prepare a path (some might call it a thread) running through the book that will allow you to shape and build the new habits that will help you become a proficient and effective storyteller.

Final Exercise

Rather than me finishing with a list or summary of what you've already seen, read and ingested, I thought I'd leave the conclusion to you.

So, let's end with one simple exercise. This book has frequently touched on the importance of memorability, so why not think about what has lingered longingly in your memory now that we've come to the end of the path?

	What I've remembered most	Why have I remembered it?	What effect did it have on me?	How I will use it?
1				
2				
3				
4				
5				
6				

ENDNOTES

1. Graham Norton, Graham Norton's Good Story Guide, BBC One, January 4, 2019

2. Elizabeth Loftus, "The 100 Most Eminent Psychologists of the 20th Century," Review of General Psychology Vol 6, No. 2 (2002): 139–152

3. Elizabeth Loftus and John Palmer, "Reconstruction of Automobile Destruction," Journal of Verbal Learning and Verbal Behaviour Vol 13, No 5 (1974)

4. Lauren Slater, Opening Skinner's Box, (New York, Norton, 2004)

5. Alison George, "I Could Have Sworn ... An interview with false-memory expert Elizabeth Loftus," Slate, last modified September 8, 2013, https://slate.com/technology/2013/09/elizabeth-loftus-interview-false-memory-research-on-eyewitnesses-child-abuse-recovered-memories.html

6. Daniel Boffey, "David Cameron Blames 'Brain Fade' for Getting His Football Team Wrong," Guardian, last modified 25 April 2015, https://www.theguardian.com/politics/2015/apr/25/david-cameron-blames-brain-fade-for-getting-his-football-team-wrong

7. Richard Dawkins, attributed

8. Dean Burnett, The Idiot Brain (London, Faber, 2016), p. 28

9. Dean Burnett, The Idiot Brain (London, Faber, 2016), p. 54

10. Dean Burnett, The Idiot Brain (London, Faber, 2016), p. 165

11. William James, Talks to Teachers (Dover Publications, 1899), Section XI

12. Everett Rogers, Diffusion of Innovation (New York, Free Press of Glencoe, 1962)

13. Russell H Colley: presented in a report to the US Association of National Advertisers (1961)

14. Green and Donahue, Handbook of Imagination and Mental Simulation (New York, Psychology Press, 2009)

15. Schreiner et al, "Argument Strength and the Persuasiveness of Stories," Discourse Processes Vol 55, No. 4 (2016): 371–386

16. Anthony Tasgal, The Storytelling Book (London: LID Publishing, 2015), p.92

17. Polly Toynbee, "If the Sun on Sunday Soars Rupert Murdoch Will Also Rise Again," Guardian, last modified 23 February, 2012

18. Francis Bacon, The Advancement of Learning (1899)

19. Anthony Tasgal, InCitations (London: LID Publishing, 2020), p. 112–3

20. Masahiro Mori, Essay (English translation), https://spectrum.ieee.org/the-uncanny-valley

21. Anthony Tasgal, The Inspiratorium (London, LID Publishing, 2018), passim

22. James Watson, cited in Steven Rose, Lifelines (Oxford University Press, 1997)

23. Steven Rose, Lifelines (Oxford University Press, 1997)

24. Attributed to the American science writer Paul Brodeur

25. Daniel Kahneman, Thinking, Fast and Slow, (New York, Farrar, Strauss and Giroux, 2011)

26. Wunderman Thompson, "Work," last accessed January 17, 2022, https://www.jwt.com/en/work/aperol-together-we-joy

27. Later attributed to the historian Arnold Toynbee

28. Anthony Tasgal, The Inspiratorium (London, LID Publishing, 2018), passim

29. Charles Handy, The Age of Unreason, (Boston, Harvard Business School, 1989)

30. Anthony Tasgal, *The Storytelling Book* (London, LID Publishing, 2015), passim

31. Andrew Stanton, "The Clues to a Great Story" (TED), last modified February 2012, https://www.ted.com/talks/andrew_stanton_the_clues_to_a_great_story. If you watch this TED talk, bear in mind that it begins with an excruciatingly funny but not wholly universally suitable joke

32. Wayne Koestenbaum, "An Interview by Christopher Hennessy," The American Poetry Review, Vol 42, No 2, https://www.aprweb.org/poems/to-be-torn-apart-is-my-ambition-an-interview-by-christopher-hennessy

33. Philip Pullman, *Daemon Voices*, (London, David Fickling books, 2017) lecture 2

34. David Mamet, *On Directing Film*, (New York, Penguin, 1991)

35. "Kurt Vonnegut on the Shape of Stories" (YouTube), last modified 30 October 2010, https://www.youtube.com/watch?v=oP3c1h8v2ZQ

36. Daniel Kahneman, *Thinking, Fast and Slow* (New York, Farrar, Strauss and Giroux, 2011)

37. David Eagleman, *Incognito* (New York, Pantheon, 2011)

38. Widely attributed to David Lynch

39. Michael Barber, "John le Carré: An Interrogation," *New York Times*, last modified September 25, 1977, https://archive.nytimes.com/www.nytimes.com/books/99/03/21/specials/lecarre-interrogation.html

40. "Kurt Vonnegut on the Shape of Stories" (YouTube), last modified 30 October 2010, https://www.youtube.com/watch?v=oP3c1h8v2ZQ

41. Martin Amis, *The War Against Cliché*, (London, Vintage, 2001)

42. Carl Jung, *Archetypes and The Collective Unconscious* (Princeton University Press, 1959)

43. Carl Jung, *Archetypes and The Collective Unconscious* (Princeton University Press, 1959)

44. Hannah Arendt, *The Human Condition*, (University of Chicago Press, 1958).

45. Anthony Tasgal, *The Storytelling Book* (London: LID Publishing, 2015); Anthony Tasgal, *The Inspiratorium* (London, LID Publishing, 2018)

46. Andy Warhol, "A Retrospective," MOMA, 1989, https://www.moma.org/documents/moma_catalogue_1815_300161087.pdf

47. Tiffany Watt Smith, *The Book of Human Emotions* (London, Wellcome Collection, 2015)

48. Robert Friedel, "Serendipity Is No Accident," *Kenyon Review*, Vol 23, No. 2 (2001): 36–47

49. Dorothy Parker (attributed)

50. Douglas Adams, *The Hitchhiker's Guide to the Galaxy* (book series: London, Pan, 1979–1985)

51. Groucho Marx,(popularised by in 1941): https://quoteinvestigator.com/2012/07/02/wonderful-party-not/

52. Emo Philips (attributed)

53. Emo Philips (attributed)

54. Quoted in Erin Strecker, "… Movie Description Goes Viral," *Entertainment Weekly*, last modified 26 October 2012, https://ew.com/article/2012/10/26/wizard-of-oz-movie-description

55. Peter Stone, "Gabriel García Márquez, The Art of Fiction No. 69," The Paris Review, accessed 25 November 2021, https://www.theparisreview.org/interviews/3196/the-art-of-fiction-no-69-gabriel-garcia-marquez

56. Tim Groenland, "The Poetics of the Sentence: Examining Gordon Lish's Literary Legacy," Irish Journal of American Studies, accessed January 19, 2022, http://ijas.iaas.ie/the-poetics-of-the-sentence-examining-gordon-lishs-literary-legacy/

57. Gordon Lish, ibid.

58. Tim Groenland, "The Poetics of the Sentence: Examining Gordon Lish's Literary Legacy," Irish Journal of American Studies, accessed January 19, 2022, http://ijas.iaas.ie/the-poetics-of-the-sentence-examining-gordon-lishs-literary-legacy/

59. Harold Brodkey, "His Son, In His Arms, In Light, Aloft," *Esquire*, last modified August 1, 1975, https://classic.esquire.com/article/1975/8/1/his-son-in-his-arms-in-light-aloft

60. Gordon Lish, ibid.

61. Reproduced in Amy Hempel, "The Harvest," *PIF Magazine*, last modified September 1998, https://www.pifmagazine.com/1998/09/the-harvest

62. Gordon Lish, ibid.

63. Robert B Cialdini, "What's the Best Secret Device for Engaging Student Interest? The Answer Is in the Title," *Journal of Social and Clinical Psychology* Vol 24, No. 1 (2005): 22–29

64. Anthony Tasgal, *The Storytelling Book* (London: LID Publishing, 2015) and JJ Abrams, "The Mystery Box," Ted talk, 2007, https://www.ted.com/talks/j_j_abrams_the_mystery_box?language=en

65. Sigmund Freud, *The Theme of The Three Caskets*, 1911, https://www.sas.upenn.edu/~cavitch/pdf-library/Freud_ThreeCaskets.pdf

66. Karl Popper, *The Logic of Scientific Discovery*, (London, Routledge, 1959)

67. For example, in *The Economist*, December 4, 2003

68. George Miller, "The Magical Number Seven, Plus or Minus Two: Some Limits on Our Capacity for Processing Information," *Psychological Review* Vol 63, No. 2 (1956): 81–97

69. Nelson Cowan, "The Magical Mystery Four: How Is Working Capacity Limited, and Why?" *Current Directions in Psychological Science* Vol 19, No. 1 (2010): 51–57

70. Anthony Tasgal, *The Storytelling Book* (London: LID Publishing, 2015)

71. Billy Perrigo, "'Get Brexit Done.' The 3 Words that Helped Boris Johnson Win Britain's 2019 Election," *Time*, last modified December 13, 2019, https://time.com/5749478/get-brexit-done-slogan-uk-election

72. Gary Rolfe, Dawn Freshwater and Melanie Jasper, *Critical Reflection in Nursing and the Helping Professions: A User's Guide* (Basingstoke: Palgrave Macmillan, 2011)

73. David Ogilvy, *Confessions of an Advertising Man* (New York, Atheneum, 1963)

74. Edward de Bono, *Simplicity* (London: Penguin, 1998), p. 43

75. Quoted in Jade Garrett, "AMV Unrolls Economist Poster Push," *Guardian*, last modified October 13, 2000, https://www.theguardian.com/media/2000/oct/13/pressandpublishing.advertising

76. Mike Schauer, ""At 60 Miles An Hour" Rolls-Royce Ad by David Ogilvy," Swiped.co, accessed January 19, 2022, https://swiped.co/file/rolls-royce-ad-by-david-ogilvy/

77. Daniel M Oppenheimer, "Consequences of Erudite Vernacular Utilized Irrespective of Necessity: Problems with Using Long Words Needlessly," *Applied Cognitive Psychology* Vol 20, No. 2 (2006): 139–156

78. Joseph Serna, "Big Rig Carrying Fruit Crashes on 210 Freeway, Creates Jam," *Los Angeles Times*, last modified May 20, 2013, https://www.latimes.com/local/lanow/la-me-ln-big-rig-crash-20130520-story.html

79. Katie Morley, "Marmalade Is the Preserve of the Elderly, Data Show," *Daily Telegraph*, last modified February 23, 2017, https://www.telegraph.co.uk/news/2017/02/23/marmalade-preserve-elderly-data-shows

80. Vincent A Musetto, "Headless Body in Topless Bar," *New York Post*, April 15, 1983

81. Charlie Carillo, "In Case You Missed It, Here's a De-Cap: Headless Body in Topless Bar!" (*HuffPost*), last modified January 25, 2012, https://www.huffpost.com/entry/in-case-you-missed-it-her_b_1229112

82. "Drugs Win Drug War," *The Onion*, January 10,1998

83. Tom Banks, "David Pearson Designs New Series of George Orwell Books," *Design Week*, last modified January 8, 2014, https://www.designweek.co.uk/issues/january-2014/david-pearson-designs-new-series-of-george-orwell-books

ACKNOWLEDGEMENTS

Thanks as ever to Martin for support and to Aiyana for labouring through the edits.

To Nikki, Josh, Zach and Saskia for everything from cheery support to benign indifference.

But most of all to everyone in the background who came to the foreground when it mattered most.

ABOUT THE AUTHOR

Anthony Tasgal is a man of many lanyards: he runs his own training company and is a Course Director for the CIM (Chartered Institute of Marketing), the Market Research Society, the Institute Of Internal Communication, the AAR (ad agency/client relationship advisers) and the Civil Service College, running courses on storytelling, behavioural economics, insightment and creative briefing in the UK, US, Europe, China, Hong Kong, Australia and UAE.

Tas is also a long-term Ad Agency planner and still freelances with several agencies and clients.

Besides this, he is an Associate Lecturer at Bucks New University and Nottingham Trent Universities and a Principal Advisor for CIO Connect in Hong Kong, the premier advisory service dedicated to CIOs and other tech leaders in HK.

Tas regularly appears on TalkRadio's Early Breakfast show to discuss marketing and advertising topics.

He is the author of *The Storytelling Book*, the award-winning guide to using storytelling techniques to improve presentations and communication, which has sold over 30,000 copies globally. His second book, *The Inspiratorium*, was a compendium of insight and inspiration, followed in 2020 by *Incitations*, a collection of expressions, phrases and words designed to incite insight.

 @tastasgal

🐦 @taswellhill

📷 @tastasgal

BY THE SAME AUTHOR

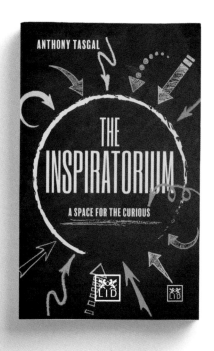

£9.99/$14.95
ISBN: 978-1-911498-46-9

INCITATIONS

DISCOVERING A WORLD OF
INSPIRATION THROUGH QUOTES,
WORDS AND EXPRESSIONS

ANTHONY TASGAL
BESTSELLING AUTHOR OF *THE STORYTELLING BOOK* AND *THE INSPIRATORIUM*

£12.99/$19.95
ISBN: 978-1-912555-57-4

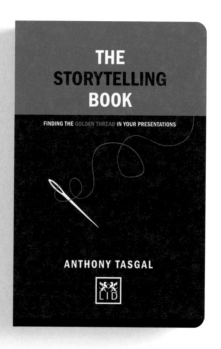

£9.99/$14.95
ISBN: 978-1-910649-08-4